CRIME AND PUNISHMENT IN THE OLD FRENCH ROMANCES

CRIME AND PUNISHMENT IN THE OLD FRENCH ROMANCES

BY

F. CARL RIEDEL

AMS PRESS, INC.
NEW YORK
1966

Reprinted 1966
with permission of Columbia University Press

AMS PRESS, INC.
New York, N.Y. 10003

Manufactured in the United States of America

To P. A. R.

ACKNOWLEDGMENTS

I OWE much to William W. Lawrence, Professor Emeritus of English, Columbia University. By a remark in one of his lectures he not only suggested the subject of this study to me, but he also guided the development of the work in its formative stages. Professor Roger S. Loomis, also of Columbia University, has likewise given generously of his time and criticism. My chief debt is to Professor Julius Goebel, Jr., of the Columbia School of Law, whose aid in questions of legal history has been invaluable, and in whose office I have spent many hours in going over material made available to me through the kindness of his assistant, Mr. Donald Tilton. Dr. Merriam Sherwood of Columbia University and Dr. Elmer Mantz of Cooper Union have offered many useful suggestions. I wish also to thank Professor William G. Crane of The College of the City of New York, Professor Floyd S. Lear of the Rice Institute, and Miss Matilda L. Berg of the editorial staff of the Columbia University Press. These people have all helped me in ways too numerous to mention.

The following have kindly permitted me to quote copyrighted material: John Byrne & Co., publishers of Beames's translation of Glanvill's *De legibus et consuetudinibus regni Angliae;* E. P. Dutton & Co., Inc., publishers of Comfort's translation of the romances of Chrétien de Troyes and of Macdevitt's translation of Caesar's *Commentaries;* Harper & Brothers, publishers of Lea's *History of the Inquisition in the Middle Ages;* Henry Holt & Co., publishers of Krehbiel's translation of Luchaire's *Social France at the Time of Philip Augustus* and of Dow's translation of Seignobos's *The Feudal Regime;* Lea Brothers & Co., publishers of Lea's *Superstition and Force;* Little, Brown & Co., publishers of Bell's translation of Bar's *History of Continental Criminal Law* and of Simpson's translation of Esmein's *History of Continental Criminal Procedure;* and the Macmillan Co., publishers of Lawrence's *Shakespeare's Problem Comedies.*

F. Carl Riedel

New York, N.Y.
June 13, 1938

CONTENTS

CRIME AND PUNISHMENT IN THE OLD FRENCH ROMANCES

I

INTRODUCTION

Por remembrer des ancessours
Li fez e li diz e li mours,
Deit l'en li livres e li gestes
E li estoires as festes,
Li felonies de felons,
E li barnages de barons.
—*Roman de Rou*

IN SPITE of Wace's suggestion that in order to enrich our knowledge of the deeds and customs of our ancestors we ought to learn something of their crimes as well as their virtues, the subject of crime and punishment as represented in the Old French romances is one that appears to have escaped the attention of most writers and commentators on medieval literature. Those who have written on it, like Pfeffer[1] and Foerster,[2] have concerned themselves chiefly with single forms of procedure or punishment, such as the judicial duel or death by fire as illustrated in the romances. And what Schultz has to say is buried in the bulk of his two-volume work, *Das höfische Leben*. Even Junge's dissertation, *Über Gerichtsbeamte und Gerichtsverhältnisse in der Litteratur des alten Frankreichs,* though useful because in some ways it is more comprehensive, refers to only two of the romances brought up for discussion in the following chapters. The present study, therefore, though not exhaustive, seems justified.

From the romances read and recited to courtly audiences we can get not only an idea of the type of entertainment that lords and ladies enjoyed, but also a notion of what they considered right and wrong, just and unjust; we can learn something of the fascination that wickedness in literary form had for them, and even something of the technique that poets exercised in handling crime and criminals. We should like to follow the course of high-handed villainy and its dire consequences with as much interest as our forebears had in it, but there are times when our ignorance of twelfth and thirteenth century life, customs, and laws is not entirely enlightened by these narrative poems. We must turn to actual histories and to the actual laws of the age in order to complete our knowledge of what a medieval audience understood or took for granted. In the following pages, therefore, after outlining the legal conditions of the period, we shall compare the romances with the actual law, and then proceed to a discussion of the social or moral aspect of the age, since moral and legal classifications are rarely identical. This will naturally lead to the question of literary influences, for there may be something of interest in learning whether the criminals of the romances conduct themselves morally as self-sufficient individuals independent of plot or whether they are merely disguised stock types borrowed from other literary forms.

The chief principle that guides the selection of the twenty-odd romances to be examined is that of realism—fidelity to the life of twelfth and thirteenth century France in general and, in particular, fidelity to the criminal law of the period. A number of romances have been rejected because, while they illustrate crime and punishment of various sorts, the treatment of this material is not legalistic and the material itself is either too fantastic for serious discussion here, or else prosaically duplicates some of the material already chosen. Although there is no special group of romances which may be labeled romances of crime, there is no valid reason why the principle of selection just mentioned should not cut across the lines of more or less recognized literary groupings. As a matter of fact, however, there is not a great degree of literary dissimilarity among the romances selected, for about two-thirds of them belong to what are called the society romances,[3] and most of the rest to what are called *romans d'aventure*.[4] The romances to be examined—all of them characteristically representative of their time—are listed below in the order in which they are brought up for discussion; in listing with them their approximate dates there has been no attempt to go beyond the limits already set by the editors and commentators.

Durmart le galois. The editor says that the manuscript in which *Durmart* was found dates from the reign of Saint Louis; Faral (in Bédier and Hazard, *Histoire de la littérature française illustrée*, I, p. 38) narrows this down to the first third of the thirteenth century, but U. T. Holmes (*A History of Old French Literature from the Origins to 1300*, p. 280) prefers the second quarter of the century.

Le Roman de la violette (p. lvii), 1227-29.

Floriant et Florete. The editor (p. ix) dates the poem in the fourteenth century, but Faral (in Bédier and Hazard, *op. cit.*, p. 38) suggests the second half of the thirteenth century. Holmes does not appear to mention this romance.

Le Roman du Comte d'Anjou (p. vi), 1316.

Sone de Nansai. The editor says nothing of the date, and Langlois (*La Vie en France au moyen âge*, I, p. 286) merely calls it the most recent of the *romans d'aventure*. J. D. Bruce (*The Evolution of Arthurian Romance*, I, p. 350), however, suggests the latter part of the thirteenth century, and Holmes (*op. cit.*, p. 276) the second half of the century.

Meraugis de Portlesguez (p. lxv), c. 1215.

Yder (p. ciii), 1223-25.

Claris et Laris (p. 863), 1268.

Blancandin. Foerster (in *Richars li biaus*, p. xxi) suggests the last quarter of the thirteenth century.

Fergus. Holmes (*op. cit.*, p. 279) suggests c. 1216.

Richars li biaus (p. xxi), last quarter of the thirteenth century.

La Manekine (p. xxi), 1270-80.

Joufrois (p. iii), beginning of the thirteenth century. Holmes (*op. cit.*, p. 274) puts it about the middle of the century.

The Erle of Toulouse. A Middle English romance adapted (Hibbard, *Medieval Romance in England*, p. 36) from a lost French original probably of the late twelfth or early thirteenth century.

Le Comte de Poitiers. Holmes (*op. cit.,* p. 271) places it in the first quarter of the thirteenth century.

Guillaume de Dole (p. lxxxvi), 1199-1201. Holmes (*op. cit.,* p. 270) says 1210-14.

Li Châtelain de Coucy. Langlois (*op. cit.,* p. 227) suggests c. 1285.

Cléomadés. Voretzsch (*Introduction to the Study of Old French Literature,* p. 399) puts it after 1275; Holmes (*op. cit.,* p. 277) says 1274-82.

Yvain (Foerster, 1906 ed., p. xiv), 1173. Holmes (*op. cit.,* p. 168) cites F. E. Guyer, who sets the date at 1166-67.

Rigomer. Neither the editor nor Holmes mentions the date, but it may be early thirteenth century.

Gilles de Chin. Faral (in Bédier and Hazard, *op. cit.,* p. 41) says that the poem is ordinarily dated about 1250 but that it may be a half century older.

Ille et Galeron (p. xx), 1167.

Guillaume de Palerne (p. xxii), late twelfth or early thirteenth century.

NOTE: Whenever a romance is cited in this study, special care has been taken to see that the narrative situation is made clear at the point of reference. Often, however, a single incident or episode may be cited in various places for different purposes. To keep the thread of narrative unbroken, those readers unfamiliar with the romances may therefore find helpful the few résumés in the Appendix following Chapter VI—résumés which to the advanced student of medieval literature may appear somewhat repetitious, especially since they retell the stories of some of the better known romances.

The romances presented above are not arranged in the order of their importance to our study; some of them are to be discussed repeatedly and at length, others are not; moreover, there will be references to a few romances not even listed. It so happens that only one verse is cited from the earliest romance mentioned, *Ille et Galeron,* 1167; on the other hand, *Le Comte d'Anjou,* 1316, the latest, receives much fuller comment. Between 1167 and 1316 lies a period of nearly one hundred and fifty years, the greater part of which falls in the thirteenth century, when perhaps three-quarters of these romances were being written.

The thirteenth century saw also the compiling of local laws in the form of half a dozen important custumals, the first of which was the *Très ancien coutumier de Normandie* (1194-1204, 1218-23); then followed in order the Norman *Summa de legibus* (1254-58), Pierre de Fontaines' *Conseil à un ami* (1254), the *Jostice et de plet* of Orléans (1260), the *Établissements de Saint Louis* (1273), and Philippe de Beaumanoir's *Coutumes de Beauvaisis* (1280-83). If in the following pages Beaumanoir's *Coutumes* is referred to more often than the other custumals, it is not because there is a conscious attempt to minimize their value—it cannot be denied that the *Très ancien coutumier de Normandie,* for instance, representing one of the largest and most powerful feudatories of all France, is in its way as important as any. In Beaumanoir's work, however, one finds a wealth of illustrative material not always present in the other custumals. Beaumanoir himself, moreover, is interesting as one of the outstanding personalities of the thirteenth century; he has in fact been called the first great jurisconsult of France.[5] For these reasons, therefore, we may in a sense consider Beaumanoir our chief legal authority, just as Andreas Capellanus has often been regarded as the chief authority on the subject of courtly love. All the compilations mentioned, however, are extremely helpful not only to the legal historian but also to anyone who wishes to acquire a comprehensive background for a study of crime and punishment in the romances.

Chapter II, while far from being a complete history of criminal law in twelfth and thirteenth century France, is an outline of legal conditions which stresses features especially significant for an understanding of the romances. In the account of organized justice or of the courts, of vengeance and private warfare, of criminal procedure, and of punishment, there is little material not available in any good legal history. Since in the romances the term *treason* conveys many different meanings, it has seemed advisable to include in the outline an attempted definition of the term together with its implications.[6]

In spite of the repeated admonition that the romances to be discussed are for the most part realistic in tone, their treatment of crime and punishment may seem, even in the light of Chapter II, a little fantastic to the modern reader. This is only natural, not only because we are dealing with the literature of an age seven centuries removed from us in time, but also because the romances themselves are essentially fiction. Although the men who wrote these narrative poems were therefore under no compulsion to make them legally accurate, we shall find them adhering remarkably close to contemporary law. Chapter III, then, does not propose to furnish an exhaustive catalogue of crime and its concomitants in the romances so much as to illustrate and explain them by reference to custom and precedent, or to what at some former time had actually been custom and precedent, for some of the romances purport to be historical.

The term *contemporary* is necessarily used here in its most elastic sense, for in paralleling the romances to the actual law, we shall find that while some aspects of custom and law undoubtedly changed from decade to decade, others remained practically the same as they had been in Carolingian or even Merovingian times. Such changes as took place probably left the basic principles of criminal law intact, at least for the romance writers, with the possible exception of one or two like Beaumanoir, who was jurist as well as poet. Thus it may become necessary, for instance, to explain similar features in two romances written perhaps a hundred years apart by referring to a *contemporary* custumal falling halfway between them in time. Conversely, it may also be necessary to refer to two custumals written three-quarters of a century apart to explain something in a romance lying between them in time. But occasionally it is impossible, even by the greatest stretch of the imagination, to regard a custom of the romances as contemporary with thirteenth century law. In such cases we can hardly deny medieval poets the privilege of conscious archaizing. It seems unnecessary, however, to go so far afield as to the Code of Hammurabi for a parallel to the romances, as Miss Matulka has done in her book on the novels of Juan de Flores.[7] But it is not altogether inconceivable that romance writers like Adenet le Roi, for example, might utilize such custom as is described in Caesar's *Commentaries,* for it is known that medieval scholars, John of Salisbury among them,[8] read Caesar with considerable interest. In view of difficulties similar to those described above, we shall find it almost impossible, except in cases like Beaumanoir's, to establish as strictly and precisely contemporary the chronology of the romances and that of the custom-data they reveal.

Likewise, except in rare instances, the futility of trying closely to associate custom and romance geographically is obvious, for there could have been little to prevent a poet from laying the scene of his romance in one country or part of a country and drawing his law and custom from another.[9] Even the custumals themselves were not mutually exclusive in respect to geographical limitations, for they not only stemmed from the same common Germanic source, the Salic Law,[10] but they even borrowed from one another. As Vinogradoff points out,[11] Beaumanoir, who compiled the custom and usages of the county of Clermont in Beauvaisis, a tiny speck on the map of northern France, often took illustrative material from the customs of neighboring lordships or even from the common law of the kingdom of France. We cannot therefore expect the ordinary romancer, in his treatment of crime and punishment, to be any more exact geographically than he is chronologically. Taking fully into consideration the difficulties mentioned above, we may restate the aim of Chapter III as follows: to show that the roots of the law and custom in the fictitious romances are, like a good deal of all fiction, deeply imbedded in the fertile soil of fact.

What has just been said about time and place in regard to the material of Chapter III applies also to Chapter IV. But whereas Chapter III is concerned more specifically with the legal side of crime and punishment in the romances, Chapter IV, in illustrating from these narrative poems some of the differences between strict legality and the moral standard of the age, shows also how, in the confusion resulting from the conflict of legal and moral criteria and obligations, the principle of force, always an evil influence, actually became one of the most outstanding features of nearly all of the more important forms of human conduct.

Chapter V treats briefly of the literary aspect of crime and criminals in the romances, touching upon the individuality and the conventionality of several prominent villains and also indicating the literary function of crime in the narrative structure of the romances.

The present study, then, in bringing together and organizing in a new way some familiar and some less well-known material from the Old French romances, aims not only to be of value to the student of medieval literature, but also to make the subject of crime and punishment in the romances as interesting to the modern reader as it undoubtedly was to the lords and ladies of thirteenth century France.

II

CRIMINAL LAW IN THIRTEENTH-CENTURY FRANCE

THE structure of medieval law in France was built up chiefly on a foundation of vengeance. The system of the courts had developed partly from the attempt to control vengeance and to adjudicate breach of contract—contract which was formal or implicit. Through the passage of time organized justice gradually evolved legal concepts of what constituted the various forms of crime, outstanding among which was the concept of treason. Legal procedure had at first developed directly from the effort to regulate vengeance, though later it became characterized by a severely rigid formality. And punishment itself, which at first had been perhaps merely a legal sanction of private vengeance, became only rather late a matter of more general public concern.

In order to obtain a more adequate understanding of the complicated structure of twelfth and thirteenth century criminal law, we shall find it convenient first to describe the courts, for they not only represented organized justice, but they looked backward toward vengeance and the breach of contract, the effort to regulate which had been largely responsible for their existence; the courts, moreover, looked forward, from case to case and from precedent to precedent, toward the formulating of the legal concepts of crime, particularly the concept of treason, which, as we shall see, had much to do with the breach of contract just mentioned. From the courts as our central point, then, we may branch out to an explanation of vengeance and a definition of treason, continuing with a discussion of criminal procedure and concluding with an account of punishment.

Organization of Justice

During the feudal age justice[1] was characterized by a confusion inherited from the Frankish period, at the close of which there had been in existence six different kinds of jurisdictions which gradually decreased to four in the twelfth and thirteenth centuries; these were the seignorial, the royal, the municipal, and the ecclesiastical jurisdictions.[2] Of these four we need concern ourselves with really only one, the seignorial, for the seignorial and the royal were in many ways alike, the chief difference being perhaps one of degree rather than kind. An additional reason for describing seignorial justice in some detail is that it was the most common and the most important since it was the justice of customary law.

The seignorial court developed chiefly out of the Frankish *mallum*. Under the Merovingians justice was rendered orally in public under the open sky, preferably upon an elevated place called the *malberg,* but later often at the gate of the chateau. The *mall* (<*mathl, mathljan*)[3] consisted of three divisions: first, a president, who was either a royal appointee known as the *thunginus,* or the count, a regular royal officer; second, a minimum number of seven freemen who acted as *rachimbourgs* or judges; and third, the *sagibarons,* agents of execution, who were soon replaced by the *vicarii* of the count. The *thunginus* perhaps merely directed the debates, caused witnesses to be heard, invited the *rachimbourgs* to deliberate and to vote, and, finally, he delivered the sentence they imposed. The count, on the other hand, had become a veritable *judex publicus* who probably performed all the duties of the *thunginus* and in addition passed judgment with the *rachimbourgs.* There were also times when he judged alone, but this was exceptional and occurred chiefly in criminal cases where quick action was necessary to restore the peace. Later, in the eighth century, the standard and tone of the court rose considerably when Charlemagne replaced the *rachimbourgs* by *scabini* (later called *echevins*), who were chosen from those eligible for the office of *rachimbourg* and who thereafter formed a standing group of professional judges better acquainted with the law than the *rachimbourgs* had been. After the breakdown of the Carolingian Empire and during the earlier part of the feudal epoch, less care was taken in the administration of justice, and the judges of this period were often untutored and no better trained for office than the Merovingian *rachimbourgs*.

A general principle coming down from Frankish times was that all free men, noble or plebeian, had the right to be judged by their peers. But, to the end of the thirteenth century, this principle remained active for the nobles only, that is, for the fief-men and vassals of the court-keeper. In pledging homage to the seignior, the vassals at the same time promised certain services, notably military service and the service of the court. This service of the court obliged vassals to come to the seignorial court in order to be judged or to act as *echevins*. When the possessor of a fief became involved in a civil or criminal process, the court-keeper submitted his case to the man's peers or co-vassals. Vassals occasionally found the court service somewhat burdensome, for in twelfth and thirteenth century France it was both binding and dangerous. It was binding because it obliged them to leave their own affairs to look after those of others and to make frequently lengthy journeys in order to reach the suzerain's court; and it was dangerous because, if one of the litigants challenged the validity of the judgment, the judges had to defend their sentence by force of arms. In order not to render the required court service too onerous, the court-keepers convoked their courts only three times a year, usually at the three great festivals, Christmas, Easter, and Pentecost.

The French seignorial court was composed, then, of two divisions: the vassals, who, like the Frankish *rachimbourgs,* were really the judges, and the court-keeper, who presided, but who in the thirteenth century could require his bailiff or seneschal to sit in his place. But the president, either court-keeper or seneschal, could not direct the debates nor could he take part in the elaboration of the judgment, which was the work of the peers. He merely received their opinions and delivered the sentence. This is why, if a judgment were questioned, the dissatisfied pleader challenged the peers and not the presiding officer.

As already pointed out, the royal feudal court was very much like the seignorial court, the king choosing his counsellors from high men of the realm—the bishops, the princes, the aristocracy, or the vassalage in general.

Of all royal court officers the most prominent was the grand seneschal,[4] who inherited his powers from the former mayor of the palace and the former count of the palace. His official title was first mentioned in an act of the year 1047. The seneschal or *dapifer* of the Capetian court had retained the service of the table at the same time that he had acquired new and extraordinary powers. As a matter of fact, he was the second personage of the realm, a sort of vice-king who acted during the absence or default of the monarch. As intendant-general he had under his orders all the personnel of the table service, and in administrative capacity he supervised and directed the provosts. He exercised in part the judicial authority which had formerly belonged to the count of the palace, but he shared it with the chancellor and at times with the other great officers of the court. At the end of the eleventh century the seneschal acquired a new power in becoming general-in-chief of the army; the office had formerly belonged to the chamberlain.

The seneschal lost his administrative power and his rights over the provosts, however, when the grand bailiffs were organized about the year 1180. Under Philip I the conflicts between the grand seneschal and the king became frequent, especially when the former wished to make his office hereditary. Becoming alarmed at the excessive authority assumed by the *dapifer,* Philip suppressed entirely the dignity of the grand seneschal in 1191 and left the office vacant. At the same time the powers of the constable were correspondingly increased. The marshal, like the constable, presided at certain judicial duels under commission from the king, while the viscount presided over regional courts under royal jurisdiction.

Vengeance

At this point the subject of organized justice may be set aside in order to discuss its rival and predecessor, vengeance[5] —a means of retribution very widespread and ancient, forming as it does, one of the chief sources not only of medieval criminal law, but of the laws of nearly all races of all time at some period of their development. While the law of vengeance often works in conjunction with some higher authority, there is frequently present, as we shall see, a spirit of conflict between the two. In medieval times this conflict, though fluctuating, was still in progress, with organized chastisement (represented by the state and the Church and leaning heavily on Roman law) eventually but tardily gaining the upper hand over the principle of vengeance as surviving in twelfth and thirteenth century penal law, which reveals itself as the modified but still vigorous remnant of the early customs and traditions of the Franks, the Burgundians, and other Germanic races that swept over Gaul during the decline of the Roman Empire.

By the fifth century the Germans, in formulating their laws, had had to reckon with the principle of vengeance, which in Merovingian times was invoked for murder, adultery, violation or rape of a married woman, insult to the honor of the family, violation of the dead, or robbery with flagrant delinquency. The Salic Law, far from attempting to suppress vengeance, tried nevertheless to limit it to cases in which the guilty party and his family could not pay the stipulated *wergeld,* the monetary equivalent of a human life. Merovingian kings further limited vengeance by their capitularies, thus not only supplementing custom but at the same time strengthening their own position against the nobles, who were inclined to war privately among themselves and to look askance at kingly authority as well. Finally, in the latter half of the eighth century, Charlemagne enacted statutes designed to discourage the exercise of vengeance altogether. These failed of their purpose, however, since among Germanic peoples the *faida* or feud, open to all ranks, was too widespread and traditional a custom to be thus easily suppressed. One ignored the courts and simply proclaimed against the offending person a feud characterized by acts of arson, brigandage, capture, ambush, and murder. At the close of the Carolingian epoch and during the early part of the feudal period, royal authority gradually declined while the power of the nobles correspondingly increased. The organization and administration of justice was thrown into a confused state little more advanced than that under the Merovingians, and, except during the Truce of God, internecine warfare flourished almost without let or hindrance.

The thirteenth century brought little substantial change to this crude system of retribution. Although it had now become the special legal privilege of the nobles only,[6] private warfare was still invoked, according to Beaumanoir, at the instance of "mort, mehaing, ou autre vilain cas de crime,"[7] crimes which according to his own definition might well be regarded as treason. The injured seignior could not only call upon his lineage even to the fourth degree[8] to aid him in his vengeance, but also, by reason of his seigniorage, could in addition call upon his vassals, guests, and serfs, and finally could even hire soldiers.[9] All were considered belligerents and as such were guaranteed by their seignior; that is, they were not held punishable for any homicide they might commit during the war.[10] Exempt among relatives were clerks, women, minors, bastards, pilgrims, and those sent at a distance in the service of the king.[11] Private wars were suspended by truce and ended by the attainment of vengeance[12] or by peace concluded between the parties. But in the thirteenth century this did not prevent the king, the baron, or the lord high justiciar from pronouncing a sentence against the guilty. In Normandy, for example, from the time of Philip Augustus the peace accorded to a murderer by the relatives of the victim was no guarantee that he would not be pursued by public authorities unless he also obtained the peace of the Duke. Moreover, if one of the two warring parties appealed to the courts, war was theoretically no longer possible,[13] for in the thirteenth century it was necessary to choose one or the other, war or the courts; and when one party appealed to the courts and the other persisted in making war, the latter became subject to penalties by order of the courts.[14]

In the feudal period the Church was the first to take steps toward restricting the scope of private warfare and its concomitant evils. It directed against this vicious custom two distinct measures. The first, appearing toward the close of the tenth century, was known as the Peace of God, which at all times endeavored to exempt from warfare and protect against it churchmen and church property, women, pilgrims, merchants, peasants, and their animals. Before the time of William the Conqueror the second measure, the Truce of God, had made itself manifest. In general it extended over lands, beasts, and possessions and prohibited all acts of war during weekends from sundown on Wednesday to sunrise on the following Monday; the Truce extended, moreover, from Advent until eight days after Epiphany, from the beginning of Rogation until eight days after Pentecost, and during Lent. The punishment (excommunication) for disobedience of these two measures having proved ineffective or insufficient, the bishops had begun toward the middle of the eleventh century to require all young faithful nobles over fifteen or even twelve years of age to swear support to the Peace and the Truce. Consequently there sprang up a number of popular leagues called Associations of Peace, one of the first of which was founded at the Council of Bourges in 1038; one of the most celebrated was the Confrérie de la Paix de Notre Dame (1182).[15] These associations did not hesitate to use force in subduing recalcitrant persons who, disregarding the Peace and the Truce, persisted in brigandage and private warfare. Thus these measures were the starting point for all public law enforcement.

It was not until the middle of the twelfth century that royalty became strong enough to undertake the establishment of peace in the realm. Its first efforts in this direction were combined with those of the Church; later it set up the *asseurement* and the *quarantaine-le-roi,* and finally it attempted to prohibit warfare altogether. In the thirteenth century the *asseurement* consisted of a solemn promise, given before a municipal, a seignorial, or a royal officer, to refrain from all violence toward the person requesting the *asseurement.* This promise, once given, could never be retracted. Although the *asseurement* helped greatly to lessen the number of private wars by substituting for them the authority of public justice, it was not entirely successful because frequently the opposing parties were much too proud to request such safeguard.[16] Perhaps even less effective was the *quarantaine-le-roi,* attributed by Beaumanoir[17] to Philip Augustus; it endeavored to protect from the surprise attacks of belligerents those relatives of the two warring parties who had not been present at the offense and who had not had time to prepare for defense or to request an *asseurement*. The king prohibited such attacks before the end of a forty-day legal truce, during which time the aforementioned relatives could prepare for war, request an *asseurement*, or negotiate for peace.

In spite of the efforts of both Church and state, the law of vengeance as practiced in blood feuds and vendettas diminished population and decreased nearly all forms of wealth. In 1258 Saint Louis, always hostile to judicial duels and tournaments, interdicted private warfare throughout his realm. But this prohibition was not universally accepted, for war was everywhere still considered legal. During the next century or two, similar prohibitions met with like success. The exercise of private vengeance did not give way until the feudal system itself began to crumble. It was not until 1357, when at the demand of the Estates General the dauphin Charles suppressed the payment of money compositions, and until 1439, when feudal military obligations became no longer valid, that the Roman principle of public vengeance, the suppression of crime by society, completely replaced by law the ancient principle of private vengeance.

Treason

One crime which called forth the vengeance either of individual or public justice was treason. To define this crime seems simple enough to us of today, who are accustomed to think of it chiefly as the attempt by force of arms to overthrow the government or to resist its laws. While present-day legal dictionaries appear to support this view,[18] our modern non-legal dictionaries suggest that treason may be a hydra-headed monster when they tell us that it involves the betrayal of any trust. Somewhere between these two broadly inclusive concepts, but perhaps a good deal nearer to the latter, lies the key to the definition of treason as it was understood in twelfth and thirteenth century France. The first concept corresponds roughly to that of lese majesty, a notion Roman in origin, while the second is chiefly Germanic in background. Lese majesty, consisting of all machinations against the king, and ultimately against the state in general, rested upon the principle of the veneration of an almost divine authority assumed by such self-styled god-kings as Alexander the Great, whom the Roman emperors had imitated in their insistence upon an uncompromising and deferential obedience. The basic note of reverence here is far removed from the idea of reciprocal fidelity which seems always to have formed the groundwork of Germanic relationships, whether between king and vassal, man and man, or husband and wife.[19]

In early times the Germanic family group may well have regarded murder, adultery, rape, insult—practically all acts which simultaneously menaced the solidarity of the family and set in motion the law of vengeance—as treason, a crime general in concept, private as an act, and social in significance. In later phases of its development the concept of treason widened in scope so as to include offenses against an authority which, while retaining certain features of its originally private nature, was definitely in the process of becoming public authority. Since it was natural for the Germanic idea of pledged faith to attach itself to the *comitatus,* cowardice or desertion on the battle-field became, in the age of Tacitus, not only a breaking of faith but in addition treason against land and folk—a treason which in a larger sense could be any violation of the interests of society as a whole. The jurisdiction of the state gradually increased until elemental crimes against individuals which had been offenses dangerous to society in its earlier stages, became, though important at all times, no longer so significant in the pattern of corporate state life. Hence in the period between Tacitus and Charlemagne the concept of treason came to include *Hochverrat* (high treason) as its most important form. This was especially true when public authority became centralized in one individual—the king, who finally required a special oath of fidelity from his subjects in order to maintain a closer control of crime. While undoubtedly *Hochverrat* had assimilated some characteristics of the Roman lese majesty, its basic feature, like that of the Germanic notion of treason in general, remained the breaking of a contract binding upon both parties.[20]

The sanctity of the bond between overlord and vassal survived the political upheavals of the post-Carolingian era and remained predominant throughout the feudal period, though on a basis for the most part different from that of early times when relationships, military or other, had been of a more purely personal nature.[21] Real property, the fief, had now in a sense become the foundation of feudal society, giving tangible significance to an already contractual relationship. This relationship was now newly reinterpreted and instituted through homage and fealty when, as Seignobos points out,

> the seigneur transferred his right by a solemn act; he put the vassal in possession of the fief by giving him a bit of straw, or a stick, or a lance or a glove, which symbolized the object transferred.[22]

If the vassal attacked his seignior or perpetrated some equally serious breach of contract, he lost his fief. The *Établissements de Saint Louis,* written about 1273, does not say that such an offense is treason, but suggests this by so regarding the crime of stealing from an overlord.[23] As Seignobos further indicates, the overlord in his turn was subject to forfeiture if he failed to observe the terms of the feudal agreement:

The seigneur, then, should not attack nor insult his vassal, nor seduce his wife or daughter. If he did, the vassal could release himself from his seigneur and at the same time keep the fief. The rupture was marked by an act which was the contrary of investiture; the vassal threw down the straw or the glove: this was the defy [breaking of faith].[24]

Although, according strictly to the wording of the custumals, offenses against one's immediate overlord cannot be called treason except by inference, perhaps as in Normandy[25] these offenses were grouped under such terms as *défi féodal,*[26] which marked the infraction of contract between a vassal and the seignior from whom he held directly: terms like *traditio* and *proditio* were reserved for application to treason against the duke, from whom a vassal may have held directly or indirectly, depending upon his status in the feudal hierarchy. But these are merely technical distinctions covering different aspects of the same crime, the breaking of pledged faith.

While no such faith had been formally established between men of equal rank or between men not bound by feudal ties, it was nevertheless generally understood and respected for reasons of mutual protection and public peace. In an age when private war was a common right, announcement of the severance of normal relationship by sending one's enemy—whether seignior, peer, or vassal—a glove or like symbol was strictly necessary. Failure to make formal *désfiance* or disavowal of contract or friendship before commencing hostilities was tantamount to treason, for according to the *Jostice et de plet,* written about 1260,

It is treason . . . when one strikes a man and he does not see the blow coming at all. Treason is begun at night. Treason occurs when one surprises a man and strikes him so that he cannot defend himself.[27]

It is this element of surprise and secrecy which furnishes the true meaning of the word *treason,* according to Viollet, who further says that in divers Latin documents of the

Middle Ages the word *tradere* had no other sense.[28] In the most complete definition of treason given by any of the French custumals before 1300 the element of secrecy and surprise is conspicuous and is partly explained by the words "mortally" and "hatred," which suggest not only the very tone and spirit of the private vendetta but by their context suggest also a tremendous widening of the concept of treason. The definition, written down about 1283 in the *Coutumes de Beauvaisis,* comes from the pen of the celebrated jurist and poet, Philippe de Remi, Sire de Beaumanoir, who says:

> And it is treason when one does not show semblance of hatred and one hates mortally so that because of the hatred one kills or causes to be killed, or strikes or causes to be struck even unto the extent of injury, him whom one hates treasonably.
> No murder is without treason, but treason may be indeed without murder in many cases, for murder is not without the death of a man, but it is indeed treason to strike or wound during a truce or pledge or in ambush, or to bear false testimony in order to have a man put to death, to dispossess him, to cause him to be banished, to make him hated of his liege lord, or in many other similar cases.[29]

The outstanding difference between these two definitions lies in the fact that according to the *Jostice et de plet* treason is primarily an act, evil intent or malice aforethought being secondary and merely implied; with Beaumanoir, however, the real crime is not so much the act, which is merely a result, as it is the intent or motive, the mortal hatred or malice aforethought, which he takes pains to place first and foremost before the reader's eye. Beaumanoir's definition is of particular interest because in principle it not only directly opposes the old French legal proverb, "Le fait juge l'homme," but means also that a man might be convicted and put to death merely for having attempted, even though unsuccessfully, to commit an act of treason.[30]

It is interesting to note, moreover, that while centering in secret treachery and infidelity, neither of these two definitions makes any reference whatever to the breach of contract in feudal relationships. Apparently, then, there were in the thirteenth century two kinds of treason having the breach of faith as a common feature, but in the one kind of treason this was the breaking of the pledged faith required in the feudal system, and in the other kind the breach of an extra-feudal faith that was implicit rather than formally expressed.

The preceding definitions not only do not explain high treason or lese majesty; they do not even mention it. The reasons for this were historical and political. From the fall of the Carolingian dynasty to the fourteenth century powerful feudal lords, recognizing royalty in little more than name only, dominated France and set up systems of government which they based largely upon local customs and their own prerogatives. Consequently the doctrine of lese majesty, which had already developed to some extent in the various Germanic laws during the Merovingian and Carolingian epochs, gave way to the more popular and traditional notions of treason expressed ultimately in the thirteenth century custumals already quoted.

Yet most of these custumals had been strongly influenced by Roman and canon law,[31] and, although there is little that is strikingly suggestive of lese majesty in them, they nevertheless contain the seeds of that doctrine, which flowered to maturity in the next century. The terms *traditio* and *proditio,* reserved for treason against the duke, show that while the early thirteenth century *Très ancien coutumier de Normandie* (perhaps least affected by Roman influence), had not yet arrived at a conception of lese majesty, it was nevertheless reaching toward a notion of public law—a notion according to which the duke appears more as a royal sovereign than simply as a feudal lord.[32] Beaumanoir, although not including in his definition of treason the alliance of the commoners of a city against their seignior, regards the instigators of such an alliance as traitors.[33] An offense like this, probably more political than personal in nature, is close to the principle of lese majesty. Beaumanoir and the *Établissements de Saint Louis* use the term *great treason* to designate truce-breaking. If the truce meant here is a truce sworn before the king or his officers, the failure to observe it is indeed "une des grans traisons qui soit."[34] Then, too, the number and type of cases reserved from time to time for royal jurisdiction point toward the gradual development of lese majesty, an early mention of the term itself occurring in the year 1314.[35]

Treason in thirteenth century France was not, however, to be identified with lese majesty; yet it was still more or less general in concept, as illustrated by the opening sentence of Beaumanoir's definition. Consequently, since there was less need for specification, we find actually listed as treason only about five offenses: theft from an overlord, truce-breaking, bearing false testimony with criminal intent, wounding without warning, and murder. But to these offenses Beaumanoir adds the generally inclusive phrase, "and many other similar cases," the outstanding features of which he suggests when, after telling us that between the *tricheeur* and the *traiteur* there is little difference, he defines *tricherie* as "all that which is consciously done through falsehood that one asserts as truth in order to harm another, even though one does not put to his own profit that which by trickery is gained."[36] To sum up: the fundamental concept of treason was, as we have seen, the act of secret attack and injury; Beaumanoir does not run counter to this view, but amplifies it to include secret attack and injury not purely physical in nature.

In conclusion it appears that in early times the general conception of treason in France was closely associated with the causes which set in motion the law of vengeance; and further, that this conception, which persisted down through the twelfth and thirteenth centuries as a principle of customary law, was supplemented from the beginning of feudalism by a purely feudal notion of treason, and from the close of the thirteenth century by the gradually increasing application of the Roman idea of lese majesty.

Procedure

In order best to understand the procedural treatment of criminals suspected and convicted of treason or other crimes in twelfth and thirteenth century France, we must realize that the motives of justice were somewhat different from those of today. The real function of the law was at first not so much to discover and convict the evil-doer as to moderate between two opposing parties, to prevent ungoverned reprisals, and to bring the warlike opponents to peaceful terms by seeing the guilt correctly placed and the guilty party properly punished.

Among the early Franks criminal procedure, which at first pertained chiefly to the individual, but which became more and more a matter of public concern as time progressed, developed largely from the required observances of restrictions and regulations increasingly imposed upon the law of vengeance, in the exercise of which the victim or a member of his family acted as the executer of the death penalty. The victim had, nevertheless, to observe certain requisite forms or be punished accordingly; he had to kill the accused in public or in broad daylight and then expose the corpse of the guilty in order that the fact be made public so as to prevent any suspicion of crime on his part. The Salian Frank placed the body upon a scaffold or suspended it from a gibbet, or else he cut off the head and exposed it upon a stake at the roadside. The Ripuarian called witnesses, told them of the homicide he had committed in virtue of his right of vengeance, and exposed the body of the criminal upon a scaffold at the crossroads.

Even when justice became better organized, the individual still took an important part in the procedure; it remained his duty to summon the accused, but he had to call upon the count to execute the sentence. An edict of Chilperic was influential in preventing the count's power from being put in motion merely by the solemn act of the plaintiff; a judgment of the *rachimbourgs* became necessary. Thus the authority of the judges grew at the expense of the pleader; public jurisdiction gradually replaced that of the individual, and the judges took a more active part in the procedure while the plaintiff no longer had direct recourse to the means of execution.[37]

In spite of the introduction of the writing down of judgments and court records,[38] the procedure nevertheless remained oral and severely formal for a very long time. This was particularly so throughout practically all of the feudal period, when members of the seignorial court were selected from among vassals few of whom were much better prepared for office than the Merovingian *rachimbourgs*.

In the twelfth and thirteenth centuries the courts imposed very strict rules upon litigants in order to lighten the burden upon the intelligence of the judges, in order to prevent fraud, and in order to profit through the errors of unwary and inexperienced pleaders. According to the *Très ancien coutumier de Normandie,* for example, simple folk knelt down to take an oath without awaiting the order from the judge (the term *judge* used in the singular ordinarily indicates the presiding officer rather than the real judges, the *echevins*). Upon perceiving their error, they rose at once, again without the judge's order, thus committing a second error, and the clerk recorded the fines on his parchment. Norman d'Orgierville, quoted in the compilation, compares this formality with a child's game in which any boy gets his face blackened if at the cry, "Now up, Bernard," he does not immediately leap to his feet.[39] Furthermore, to quote Bar,

> A defendant especially ran great risk, from the beginning of his trial; in fact, he was obliged, upon pain of a fine, if ordered by the judge, to answer word by word the charge formulated against him; he even risked falling "in misericordiam curiae," which gave ground for a discretionary fine, so that, in strictness, the lord would have the right to seize all his personal property. If the defendant wished to plead an excuse, he could do so only after making an answer, or, at least, together with his answer.[40]

The accused was required to answer to the charge, for silence was regarded as a confession. When the defendant uttered a formal denial, the *echevins* made an interlocutory judgment on the manner of proof the accused must furnish.[41]

Apropos of such rigid formalism in which each word had its weight, Beaumanoir says that since many people do not know the customs nor how to maintain legal processes, they may have the assistance of an *avocat* or counsel.[42] This counsel, to begin with, was not always a professional legal man, but could be simply a friend or relative of the defendant,[43] but one, of course, who knew a little more about the law. He could not only speak in place of the defendant, but, by agreement with him, could deny, alter, or amend a statement of the latter. The defendant could likewise amend or deny a statement made by his representative, but he was advised not to do so.[44] While these privileges to a certain extent broke the rigidity of the word-for-word formalism, they merely shifted some of the responsibility from the pleader to his *avocat* or *avant-parlier,* who had to take care not to go beyond his powers and especially not to lose his temper.[45]

Thus, because of the risks involved, the defendant avoided litigation as much as possible; on the other hand, the plaintiff, according to Esmein,[46] often hesitated to accuse the criminal formally because of inertia, fear, or corruption. Although the severe formality of procedure had been designed primarily to prevent fraud on the part of either defendant or plaintiff, it often recoiled against the innocent and assisted in the machinations of the wicked. Esmein points out that

> The chances of impunity flowing from this system are still further enhanced both by the publicity which exists in all phases of the procedure and by the necessity which compels the judge to limit his investigation to the evidence furnished him by the accuser.[47]

The fact that evidence, of a certain type, is thus virtually limited to that produced by the plaintiff is, on the other hand, very much in the false accuser's favor and may serve to explain the conviction of many an innocent person in real life as well as in the romances. So frequent did false accusation become in the Middle Ages that custumals like the *Établissements de Saint Louis* borrowed a measure from Roman law designed to curb it; namely, that the accuser and the accused must both remain in prison until one or the other is proved guilty.[48]

Like the rest of the procedure the proof was essentially formal and characterized by insecurity and openness to corruption. When a person was not actually found in the deed, when guilt was not self-evident, or when presumption failed to convince, the courts resorted to the use of what were known as judgments of God, really pagan ordeals in which the elements of force, superstition, and chance dominated but which, since the people would not give them up, the Church, though protesting against their use, took over and endued with awe-inspiring ceremony. We ought, perhaps, to make a certain distinction between the judgments of God and the other forms of proof. The finding of a person in a criminal act, or the presumption of his guilt based upon certain kinds of evidence was for the most part considered as proof favoring the accuser; nevertheless, it was at times regarded as grounds for the immediate exercise of the right of vengeance or merely as grounds for accusation—in many cases real proof, or what was called real proof, lay in the ordeal or in the combat.[49] In early times such proof was considered a right and a duty of the defendant[50] and at the same time was regarded as an advantage because its outcome was largely dependent upon the physical strength or the will power of the person making the proof. It was always possible, on the other hand, that justice, acting upon a strong presumption of guilt, was apt to make the chances of success in a judgment of God nearly impossible. Unless the defendant had no defense or unless he permitted the judge to grant the privilege to the plaintiff, the latter had no right to make proof. And according to Beaumanoir, if whoever had to prove failed in one manner of proof, he had recourse to no other method.[51]

We may now take up the various proofs in brief detail, beginning with those in which the law attempts to solve its problems by logic and concluding with cases settled, after reason has reached an impasse, by the risky and dangerous ordeals. The intricacy of medieval reasoning is usually difficult for the modern reader to grasp. One's head fairly swims at the speculation of what the result might have been, had the schoolmen applied their systems of formal logic entirely to contemporary law instead of chiefly to theology.[52] But even without the subtleties of scholasticism the logic of twelth and thirteenth century law is not easy to follow.

If a man were found in a criminal act, the discovery alone was sufficient proof of his guilt. No one even today has any quarrel with this principle. But in the Middle Ages there was a strong tendency to accept in place of fact inference based upon false logic. Circumstantial evidence was often given undue prominence. Only rather late does the law clarify itself on this point. In the case of adultery, for example, Beaumanoir, while granting the husband the right to take the life of his wife and that of her lover if he finds them in the deed, stipulates emphatically that simply finding them in the same room together is insufficient evidence of their crime.[53] But if any one were actually taken in flagrant delinquency of whatever nature, his death was almost inevitable, for in earlier times, in the presence of a sufficient number of witnesses, it was lawful to dispatch him on the spot; and in the thirteenth century when a person was taken in the act, an accuser was unnecessary and the wager of battle could not be evoked. The court-keeper, surrounded by his men, before whom his sergeants brought the guilty party, judged him at once in public, according to the testimony of those who had seized him.[54] In the event that the offender escaped or that the injured party was unable to seize him without aid, the customary procedure required him to utter a loud cry in order to give publicity to the crime and to call neighbors or vassals to assist in the taking of the criminal. This obligation of the cry was the procedure known as the *clameur de haro*,[55] a humorous instance of which we have in Chaucer's *Nun's Priest's Tale* when the poor widow and her two daughters vociferously shout, "Out! harrow! and weylawey! Ha! ha! the fox!"

While the finding of a criminal in the act constitutes what today we should call proof by witness, what the Middle Ages understood as proof by witness not only differed in several respects but was not regularly used in criminal law.[56]

A manner of proof very much used in the twelfth and thirteenth centuries, however, was that which Beaumanoir calls the proof of clear presumption,[57] which at times offered excellent opportunity for the exercise of false logic. The jurist recognizes this fact and hence suggests that

This sort of proof may have many forms, for some can give the fact so clearly that it is proved by the presumptions, and others are so doubtful that misdeeds cannot be proved by them.[58] [Although Beaumanoir warns others of this pitfall, he himself is the first to fall into it, for he says:] The second form of clear presumption which is so clear that it is equal to proof, is when a threat is made, and after the threat, the thing is done which was threatened.[59]

If a man threatens another with injury or death, he is held responsible should the other afterwards be found dead or wounded. In other words, it is only necessary to prove that the former has made the threat in order to prove him guilty of the crime. When one of the finest and most conservative legal minds in the entire Middle Ages reasons in this fashion, it is only natural to expect that presumption of guilt was a proof very generally relied upon. Beaumanoir further tells us, for example, that if stolen goods are found in a man's house, his crime is not apparent, for his neighbors, servants, or enemies may have placed the stolen articles there, perhaps in order to get him into trouble; but if these articles are found on his person, he is through clear presumption regarded as a manifest thief[60]—in spite of the possibility that through persuasion or malice someone may have planted the incriminating evidence upon him. In a case of this sort, if a man of good repute is found vested with stolen property and he cannot find or cause to be taken the one who has given it to him, he ought to be absolved upon rendering up the stolen goods; but if he neither can find the person who has given him such property nor has any reliable witness, he ought to be judged for theft; and for this reason, says Beaumanoir, one ought to take care how he receives things from another.[61]

Often when our ancestors became impatient of too great an expenditure of logic, they arrived at results by a short cut. With the court's consent a suspected person could clear himself of guilt merely by swearing to his innocence. In this form of proof, however, custom required him to secure a number of compurgators or oath-helpers, usually kinsmen or peers, to swear with him. Although today we are inclined to regard as somewhat doubtful a means of proof which allows prejudiced parties to swear in favor of a person whose interests concern them deeply, people in the Middle Ages for the most part had great respect for the oath in spite of its opportunities for perjury and argued that those intimately associated with the suspect were best able to pass judgment on his character. Hence, if a man's own family or his associates considered him innocent, their opinions must be based upon something more substantial than the ties of blood or friendship.[62] Custom often stipulated definite numbers of oath-helpers, depending on the nature of the case and the social position of the party involved, but this was not uniform. One of the best known instances of compurgation in the early Middle Ages was that of Queen Fredegond, who persuaded three bishops and three hundred nobles to swear to the legitimacy of her infant son.[63] This form of proof, however, fell into general disuse during the feudal period except for a few instances. The *Coutumes de Beauvaisis* and the *Établissements de Saint Louis* omit mention of it altogther, while the *Summa de legibus* speaks of it only under the term *diraisnia.*[64] But compurgation prevailed in Gascony, even in cases of murder and other crimes entailing the death penalty, until Philip the Bold suppressed it in 1280.[65] And Lea tells of its occurrence even in 1303 when Philip the Fair ordered a man to exculpate himself of the crime of murder by a purgatorial oath with ninety-nine nobles.[66]

Compurgation was not the only means of proof resorted to in the absence of evidence or whenever there was reasonable doubt concerning the defendant's guilt. In such cases the most popular proof, though, as Beaumanoir says, the most perilous, was the judicial combat, the use of which Charlemagne had urged as preferable to the shameless oaths.[67] As a means of regulating the law of vengeance the judicial duel must have been of some value, for, as Lea says,

If, therefore, the fierce warrior, resolute to maintain an injustice or a usurpation, can be brought to submit his claim to the chances of an equal combat or of an ordeal, he has already taken a vast step towards acknowledging the supremacy of right and abandoning the personal independence which is incompatible with the relations of human society.[68]

The principle involved was that which underlay all ordeals; namely, that God would sustain the righteous and put down the wicked. But as Gautier points out,

This duel, besides, was a brutal custom, a gross superstitious observance, against which at one time the voice of Agobard and those of many other priests were uplifted. What matter? Those barbarians pretended to sanctify their barbarisms, and mixed up the Deity with the interest of their anger: a strange mixture of savagery and faith which the Church was compelled to tolerate, and on which she could only confer a more elevated character.[69]

Such militant faith as this, says Lea, was immune from the lessons of common sense and experience, and endeavored to account for the repeated miscarriage of justice in the conduct of the duel by any form of reasoning except the right one. Hence a defeated combatant, though actually known to be innocent of the special offense charged, suffered supposedly in consequence of other sins because, according to a doctrine supported by papal authority as enunciated by Innocent III in 1203,[70] he was guilty in God's sight although not in man's. Thus while some combatants tried to bribe the Deity by rich gifts in order to avoid defeat, others resorted for protection to the powers of darkness. Consequently in the thirteenth century they were required, in the oath before battle, to swear not only to the falsity of their opponents' claims but also to use no charms or magic.[71] As to the first part of the oath, defeat meant not merely the loss of the suit, but also a conviction for perjury, and even in civil cases the defeated warrior was accordingly punished and debarred from acting as a witness at any subsequent time.[72] If by reason of extreme age or physical incapacity a party could not fight, or if the party were a woman or an ecclesiastic, the combat could be fought by a substitute, usually a kinsman but sometimes a hired champion.[73] When champions were employed in capital cases, both accuser and accused had to remain in prison where they could not see the combat. The rope to hang the party sponsoring the defeated champion was put around them, and if one were a woman the spade to dig her grave had to be present.[74] In less serious cases, while the principal may have got off with a fine, his defeated champion suffered the loss of a hand, according to Beaumanoir, who intimates that the hired warrior, bearing in mind this chastisement, would be less likely to betray his employer to the other side by rendering himself recreant.[75] Since in certain cases the litigant could choose his own witnesses, and since some customs required witnesses to come armed to court, a lucrative business developed for the professional warrior-witness, whose oath before battle came often to be a mere legal fiction. Yet the judicial duel survived in spite of the prohibition of Saint Louis and the restrictions of other monarchs until it died a natural death in the fifteenth and sixteenth centuries.[76]

Like most other forms of proof the ordeals were not altogether satisfactory. Yet from Carolingian times on they had been extremely prevalent in spite of vigorous protests by a few of the more intelligent men like Agobard and later Ivo of Chartres,[77] outnumbered as these men were by such zealous believers in the infallibility of the ordeals as Hincmar. The popularity of the ordeals, their support by the clergy against the opposition of popes and kings, and the discredit of proof by witness helped to prolong the life of these semi-barbaric tests through the twelfth century.[78]

Even up to 1215 in Normandy judgments by cold water and hot iron were in constant use.[79] But the absence of any reference to them in the *Établissements de Saint Louis,* the *Coutumes de Beauvaisis,* and other custumals compiled after the Lateran Council of 1215 shows that the ordeals had fallen definitely into disuse.

As may be guessed, success in some of these peculiar forms of judgment depended upon a temporary suspension of physical law. In the cold water test, for instance, the accused, bound hand and foot with cord, was lowered by means of a rope into consecrated water. If he sank, he was innocent; if he floated, he was guilty, the theory being that the pure element would not receive into its bosom the impure and sinful person.[80] Strangely enough, more miracles were demanded of the innocent than of the guilty. In order to clear himself of blame, a suspected person might be required to carry a red-hot iron weighing one to three pounds over a distance of three to nine paces; sometimes in this proof he had to walk barefoot over nine red-hot ploughshares. The test of his guilt or innocence really occurred three days later when the exposed member, which had been bandaged and sealed during this time, was examined by the priest in charge. Signs of healing showed innocence, but an aggravated condition proved guilt.[81]

It is possible that the clergy, under whose supervision these ordeals were performed, could so control conditions that the party considered innocent was permitted to escape unharmed. The ordeal was often trained for in advance, and although the use of magic was forbidden, accused persons sometimes relied upon various unguents to harden the skin, applying them to hands or feet over a period of time before the event.[82] While trickery may have assisted some people in dangerous tests, passionate faith, enthusiasm, and self-hypnosis doubtless helped to establish the innocence of many others.

Punishment

The difficulty of assigning to twelfth and thirteenth century France any one codified and well-accepted legal system will be at once apparent, for the procedure of the accusatory system alone may be said to have applied generally, and that, doubtless, with numerous exceptions. Each feudatory had its own particular custom, and while such customs may have resembled one another in their main features, they often differed in detail. Some of these differences were obviously concerned with the manner and degree of punishment inflicted upon the wrongdoer. Yet while various laws recommended definite punishments for certain crimes, these chastisements were not strictly obligatory, according to Glasson, who says that in general during the feudal period the judge enjoyed a most absolute power and could strike as he wished, that the penalties were arbitrary, and that at times the most rigorous punishments were inflicted without even the formality of a trial.[83] Such severity, however, was not universally exercised. An examination of the medieval philosophy of punishment may help to explain why justice seemed to oscillate between two extremes, unreasonable cruelty and unreasonable mercy.

The penal system owed much of its cruelty to its own foundations—the law of vengeance and the necessity of frightening criminals by the horror of corporal punishment. Even the influence of primitive religion was not entirely absent in the beginning, for the appeasement of an angry god, the purification of the land, the purging of the air, and the cleansing of the people were sufficient reasons for castigations of a cruel nature. Strange pagan rites were at the bottom of certain forms of execution: beheading was associated with the god of lightning, death by the wheel with the sun-god, drowning with the water-demons, and hanging with the wind-god.[84] Hanging, the most disgraceful of deaths, was the usual punishment for robbery, and the criminal went naked and blindfolded to the gallows—blindfolded to protect onlookers from his evil eye.[85] Prudishness and the sense of outraged dignity may have enhanced the cruelty of vengeance. Women were usually burned or buried alive, perhaps for the sake of modesty. The early Germans, according to Tacitus, punished adulteresses by shearing off their hair and whipping them out of the community, possibly to die of exposure,[86] and the West Goths whipped them and burned them alive.[87] The Burgundians drowned adulterous wives in marshes to conceal their lewdness and even pronounced the death penalty against the betrothed woman who espoused another man.[88] The Salic Franks punished the adulterer by burning him, but then only if he were a serf or a menial.[89] In order that people might see and protect themselves from lesser criminals, offenders were branded or had their ears or noses cut off.[90] Sometimes malefactors were deprived of hands or eyes in order to prevent the repetition of a crime.[91] A somewhat more commendable purpose in such severity was, according to the Burgundian law, "ut paucorum condemnatione multitudo corrigatur."[92] Generally throughout the feudal period, however, the effort to proportion chastisement to offense resulted in such brutalities as the cutting off of the perjurer's oath-hand and the writing-hand of the forger if either criminal did not suffer death; it resulted also in the burning alive of the incendiary, in boiling the counterfeiter, and in gouging out the eyes and the tongue of the spy.[93] Moreover, says Bar,

> from the twelfth and thirteenth centuries on, the increasing use of torture and the studied aggravation of punishment, effected largely through the influence of the Inquisition and Roman law, reached the last extremity—while at the same time it was generally believed that cruelty was but the performance of a task pleasing to God.[94]

It would be senseless to presume that there was never any attempt at moderation and disinterestedness in the practice of twelfth and thirteenth century justice. Such moderation and impartiality as existed, however, were applied not according to modern notions of these qualities but according to twelfth and thirteenth century versions of them. Thus the *Jostice et de plet,*[95] systematizing after the fashion of Roman law, asserts that penalties should be established according: (1) to cause, as when one strikes another; (2) to person, as when one is worthy and less given to evil-doing; (3) to place, as when one does amiss before a judge, in church, in a sacred place, at the market, or at the fair; (4) to time, as when one does amiss by day or by night, or on holy days or nights; (5) to quality, as when the deed is more or less serious or when it is done openly or in secret; (6) to quantity, as when the crime involves much or little; and (7) to chance, as when one wounds another by accident. Moreover, says the same treatise, the judge ought not to covet the glory of being too hard or too easy.

In speaking of the duties of the bailiff, Beaumanoir reveals an attitude toward the dispensing of justice generally similar to the one just indicated.

The third virtue that the bailiff ought to have is that he should be mild and easy-tempered, without violence and cruelty; and not easy-tempered among wrong-doers, nor toward the cruel, nor toward those who do misdeeds, for to such manner of people ought he to show semblance of cruelty and anger and force of justice, that their evil-doing be less. For just as the physician who, for pity of the sick man's malady fails to probe the wound of which he ought to cure him, puts him in peril of death, so also the bailiff who is easy-tempered toward the malefactors of his bailiwick puts in peril of death those who wish to live in peace; nor can a bailiff, all in all, render a greater service than to clear out the bad from the good by rigor of justice. Hence in saying that he ought to be easy-tempered, we mean toward those who wish well and toward the common people, and in cases which arise more through mischance than through malice. And because we have said that wisdom is the sovereign virtue of those which a bailiff should possess, one ought not to hold the bailiff for wise who towards all is fell and cruel. And often it happens that simple folk, who have good suits and lawful, let lose their suits because they dare not maintain them before such bailiffs on account of their [the bailiffs'] violence, for fear of losing more.[96]

In spite of careful provision for classification of crime and corresponding gradation of punishment, there is evidence, both direct and inferential, of frequent inappropriate or unwarranted chastisement. The last two sentences just quoted from Beaumanoir are borne out by the fact that in 1261 two men were hanged without trial and that in Normandy under Saint Louis the canons of Cherbourg were deprived of their rights of justice in eight criminal cases, in six of which the prisoners had been hanged before the canons could make their claim.[97] When Beaumanoir speaks disparagingly of the cowardly bailiff who does not dare to anger the rich man in his process against the poor man or who does not dare to mete out the death penalty for fear of the malefactor's relatives, we may safely infer that many a criminal got off without his just deserts because of his wealth or influence.[98] As a matter of fact, a man's wealth and social position often determined the extent of his punishment if it were in the form of a fine.[99] Sometimes the same or similar offenses resulted in startlingly different punishments. According to the *Registre criminel de Saint-Maure-des-Fossés* in 1277 a man was hanged for the theft of an egg. About a year later a man who had stolen a chicken suffered merely the loss of an ear.[100]

Although some secular custumals, ostensibly under the influence of the Church, urged that grace is better than justice and that justice without mercy is injustice, the design of bettering the criminal was at first scarcely known, and was approached only by canon law.[101] That the wrongdoer might be rehabilitated; that he might not be solely responsible for his crime, but that society might, to a certain extent, be his accomplice; and that judges might err —these sentiments were, according to Huizinga, almost unknown in the Middle Ages. Yet, as he goes on to say, all of these

> may have been implied in the very strong and direct feeling of pity and forgiveness which alternated with extreme severity. Instead of lenient penalties, inflicted with hesitation, the Middle Ages knew but the two extremes: the fulness of cruel punishment and mercy. When the condemned criminal is pardoned, the question whether he deserves it for any special reason is hardly asked; for mercy is gratuitous, like the mercy of God.[102]

The reader who remembers that *merci, misericordia curiae,*[103] and other forms of mercy gave ground for discretionary fines will be likely to question whether man's mercy was quite so gratuitous as God's. Without wilfully misconstruing the meaning of Huizinga's statement, one may readily see that certain legal and ecclesiastical interpretations of the term *mercy* involved the payment of fines and monetary penances—a fact which may have had its share in accounting for numerous inappropriate punishments. Moreover, it is probable that, in view of the arbitrary sentences often handed down by the judges, the application of extremely inappropriate punishments resulted from an indiscriminate confounding of ecclesiastical and secular theories of penology.[104] This confusion came about through the conflicting aims of state and Church regarding the disposition of the criminal, since on the one hand the state endeavored to maintain public peace through the law of the vengeance of society and the intimidation of the criminal by means of terrible punishments,[105] while on the other hand the Church aimed rather to improve the wrongdoer morally by insisting upon his complete and utter repentance.[106]

The Church, at times forgetful of the demands of society in her effort to save the soul of the sinner, had brought into existence a system of penances at first set up in opposition to the more drastic judicial sentences. These penances, which varied naturally according to the gravity of the crime, in the beginning had consisted of more or less severe fasts, the wearing of hair cloth, the assumption of humiliating posture at church, exile, degradation or deposition for clerks, and, finally, excommunication. Moreover, conforming to the remark of St. Paul, the Church made no exception of social class or of sex, and through the force of concurrent and compulsive action by civil officials, was able to inflict degrading punishments upon even the most eminent personages. The penance pronounced could be perpetual, as exile for the crime of murder. For adultery the penance was a seven-year exile for the man as well as for the woman—an equality of punishment which did not recognize the distinctions by which secular law punished erring wives almost exclusively while at the same time it permitted husbands to maintain concubines or to repudiate one wife and marry a second.[107] In cases of rape the Church insisted that a man who had ravished a virgin should either marry her or submit to the usual punishment—exile or the payment of a heavy fine—while on the other hand, secular law demanded his death.[108]

Yet, in spite of itself, the attempt at spiritual redemption through mercy and penance, while noble in conception, became actually mercenary as time progressed. This is, for example, plainly shown in the development of a form of penance widely used in the Middle Ages. In Frankish times exile, though cruel enough in the disgrace and hardship involved, was a mitigation of still more rigorous punishment. It was the Church's idea to keep the exiled person out of further mischief and at the same time to improve his morals by ordering him to visit some holy shrine, its distance depending ordinarily upon the degree of offense. Growing out of exile and at times hardly distinguishable from it, pilgrimage as punishment was, like some of the other penances, later incorporated in the secular customs, thus becoming more widespread in usage. Pilgrimage came to be an awkward business for the poor, who were forced to proceed to their destination on foot, begging alms along the road. The nobility, on the other hand, might ride on horseback unless directed otherwise. But when merchants made new business relations as they went along fulfilling their penalty, pilgrimage as punishment sharply declined in significance—a significance which had already become doubtful when the penance could be avoided altogether merely by the payment of a fine.[109]

While at first the payment of fines to avoid ecclesiastical penance or secular punishment may have been somewhat influenced by the principle of the reparation of a damage, later, when most of the money went into the coffers of the Church, the seignior, or the community instead of into the hands of the injured party, the mercenary spirit so predominated that any sincere desire not only to make the criminal a better member of society by redeeming him through grace but also to chastise him appropriately according to his crime was almost entirely lost sight of. And in view of the social and ethical mores of the age the oscillation between cruelty and mercy, whether mercy was gratuitous or not, was only to be expected. It is inappropriate to include here a more extended account of economic sanctions against criminals, as the romances, seeking dramatic effect, stress rather the punishment of the body, referring only rarely to sanctions against property.[110]

III

CRIMINAL LAW IN THE OLD FRENCH ROMANCES

IN COMPARING the criminal law of the Old French romances with the actual law of the times, we shall find it helpful to remember that our purpose is merely to show their similarity, not to make the one fit the Procrustean bed of the other. The fact that the romances themselves are fiction not only prohibits such inflexible treatment of them but also presents certain difficulties in the analysis of them. One episode in *Le Comte d'Anjou,* for example, offers an excellent illustration of the organization of both the royal and the seignorial courts; yet so compactly is this material mortised and tenoned to matter illustrating the conduct of private warfare, which might well be discussed under the heading of procedure, that they are hardly to be separated. And though the general topic of vengeance is reserved for Chapter IV, part of which discusses the relation between legal and moral standards, we shall nevertheless try here to derive some order from the crazy-quilt pattern of the romances by following as closely as possible the arrangement of subject matter in Chapter II, beginning with organized justice and continuing with treason, procedure, and punishment.

Jurisdiction, Function, and Organization of Justice

The picture of medieval law and justice as represented in the romances here under discussion, fairly accurate as far as it goes, is not a complete one, for it is easy to find in any of the custumals large sections which have no counterpart in these romances. In discussing the matter of jurisdiction and the organization and function of justice in the romances, we should realize that we have here to do with poems written, sometimes by clerks and monks, for a feudal aristocracy interested not nearly so much in learning and religion as in love and war. Consequently, in this type of literature we must expect to find kings, counts, and nobles playing more prominent roles than bishops and priests. This is particularly true in the conduct of criminal cases in the romances, for in the one episode, the heresy trial of Fenise in *Durmart,* which offers the most reason for us to expect to find canon law and the Church tribunal playing a predominant part, we are disappointed.

It is common knowledge that ordinarily in the thirteenth century the Church courts tried cases of heresy and turned heretics obstinate in their unbelief over to secular justice, which inflicted the death penalty.[1] How is it then that in *Durmart le galois,* written during the reign of Saint Louis, King Arthur's court in trying Fenise for heresy takes over a case apparently belonging under jurisdiction of the ecclesiastical courts? We may understand the situation better if we have a summary of the story to go by.

When Queen Fenise of Ireland calls her cousin and vassal, King Nogant, a coward, he retaliates by making war against her. He is successful until Durmart arrives to defend Fenise.

King Arthur then comes to Ireland at the request of Nogant, who writes falsely of Fenise that "she is a miscreant and a fool; of God she does not wish to hear a word; marriage she hates and despises, and also the sacrament of Holy Church."[2] Arthur, a little skeptical and desiring to know whether Nogant "says false or true,"[3] sends Josefent, Durmart's father, in embassy to the queen to learn her side of the case and to summon her to court. Being graciously received, Josefent tells Fenise that Arthur has come "to judge the miscreants and to advance the law of God,"[4] and promises her that if she can show the king that she is of the Christian faith, she need not fear. She goes to court and faces the repeated formal charge of Nogant before Arthur and the assembly.

"Sire, . . ." says Nogant, "so great an unbeliever is the queen whom I see here that she should not hold land . . . which . . . I should have by judgment . . . I am ready to show now that according to law she should be put to death and . . . that . . . she should be burned. . . ."[5]

Fenise flatly denies the accusation, states the facts, and says, "this the archbishops and the abbots and the bishops know well. . . ."[6]

Furthermore, she repeats the creed and offers to undergo the ordeal by fire to prove her faith. When she has finished speaking, all the people from the city, "knights and clerks and laymen,"[7] come to testify against Nogant, who, in view of the evidence and in fear of the impending duel with Durmart, absconds.

No one can help noticing the insignificant part played by the clergy in the trial. While Fenise mentions the archbishops, the abbots, and the bishops, it is obvious that at first they are not even present, for the trial is conducted solely under the auspices of King Arthur. Later, when they come to testify in behalf of Fenise, the clergy play only ordinary roles, testifying along with a crowd of knights and other laymen. What were the reasons for this apparent disregard for the authority and jurisdiction of the Church? Even if only for a partial explanation, we must examine anew the historical relations between Church and State during the twelfth and thirteenth centuries, a brief account of which is given in a note to the preceding chapter. Since the trial takes place in Ireland, we may find interesting a rough parallel in English history. It is at once significant that Henry II sought and obtained Pope Adrian's permission to enter Ireland, like Arthur in the romance, for the purpose of

> the enlargement of the Church's borders, for the restraint of vice, the correction of morals and the planting of virtue, the increase of the Christian religion, and whatsoever may tend to God's glory and the well-being of the land. . . .[8]

It is still more significant that the proposed invasion of Ireland not only took place at the request of Dermod, worsted in Irish civil war,[9] but that it also took place about the time of Henry's controversy with Becket, the reaction to whose murder did little to thwart Henry, for as a matter of fact the victory remained with the king. Furthermore, from the time of William the Conqueror no tenant in chief might be excommunicated—and his land could probably not therefore be placed under interdict—without the king's consent.[10] Although there is no way of telling whether the author of *Durmart* was aware of these historical facts, it is clear that his invention did not go beyond the bounds of reality. Had he chosen, he might have had even further precedent for his treatment of the heresy trial, for not only in Frankish times did Carolingian crown procedure combine both secular and ecclesiastical sanctions,[11] but later the *Très ancien coutumier de Normandie* provided that counts, barons, and knights of the duke's household were not to be excommunicated without the consent of the duke.[12] And even Saint Louis himself had had to refuse certain of the bishops' demands concerning excommunicated persons—demands which were, according to Joinville, "against God and reason."[13] There was, moreover, additional historical precedent for the *Durmart* poet in several parts of Italy, where under Frederick II a secular inquisition was being experimented with.[14] Such precedents were undoubtedly the results of the controversy between Church and State, in which there was a good deal of chicanery on both sides. In *Durmart,* however, no such conflict is evident; in the heresy trial the Church, subservient to the State, assumes merely a minor role, while royalty is present not only in the true interests of religion but also to see justice done to its true servants and to see that the mixture of politics and religion has no evil results—for after all, we must remember that Nogant lays claim to Fenise's lands because he says she is a heretic. Concerning this sort of thing, Lea remarks:

it was soon perceived that an accusation of heresy was a peculiarly easy and efficient method of attacking a political enemy. No charge was easier to bring and none so difficult to disprove. ... No crime, moreover, according to the accepted legal doctrine of the age, carried with it a penalty so severe for a potentate who was above all other laws.[15]

We may conclude, therefore, that though the heresy trial in *Durmart* may be pure romantic fiction, it nevertheless has a firm basis in contemporary life and practices.

What is true of the *Durmart* episode is for the most part true of all romances under discussion: namely, that while occasionally bishops and the clergy may assist in trials and while they may conduct ordeals under the auspices of the Church, they act merely as adjuncts of seignorial or royal justice; there is no outstanding illustration of the medieval ecclesiastical court in the romances, probably because in the thirteenth century most criminal cases came under jurisdiction of the secular courts,[16] the organization and functioning of which the romances copy closely. The *Roman de la violette* offers an illustration of the seignorial court in action when, in the outdoor trial of Euriaut for her supposed murder of Ysmaine, the Duke of Metz presides over twelve peers, who are to impose a judgment determining first whether Euriaut may offer proof, and, if so, then an interlocutory judgment determining the manner of proof.[17] The romance *Floriant et Florete* presents something like a royal court when the Emperor of Constantinople presides over twelve kings, who step outside the emperor's tent to decide the manner of death to be inflicted upon the wicked Maragoz, a murderer and traitor already proved guilty in a judicial duel.[18] Maragoz, it should be remarked, is judged not by his superiors but by his equals since, after having murdered his king, he himself had assumed the throne.[19] Although, in these two cases, the number of judges in the courts—twelve—exceeds the minimum by five, this fact may be attributed to an historical precedent dating from 819; at that time Louis the Pious stipulated that certain pleas were to be heard by a minimum number of twelve judges instead of the usual seven.[20] Moreover, according to Esmein, in the first third of the thirteenth century there had come into existence a judicial organization known as the twelve peers of France, six being high representatives of the Church and six being great feudal laymen.[21]

Le Roman du Comte d'Anjou, written about 1316, presents an excellent example of the relations between seignorial and royal justice, together with many interesting sidelights. The strong probability that the author was one Jehan Maillart,[22] a notary of the *Hotel du Roy* and one of the principal functionaries of the chancellery during the time of Philip the Fair and his sons, vouches for the fidelity and regularity of the description:

When the Count of Bourges's wicked aunt, the Countess of Chartres, forges letters demanding the death of her nephew's wife and child, the men who are to carry out the supposed order of the count take pity on them and send them out of the country as exiles instead. The count, upon learning what has happened, searches far and wide before he at last finds his wife and child. Naturally, then, he wishes to wreak vengeance upon his aunt,[23] but first he asks counsel of his men. They advise him to seek the *accort du roy*[24] of the King of France, his cousin, in order that the affair might go according to "legal procedure without peril and without penalty."[25] The king himself, after seeking counsel of his own advisers,[26] summons the wicked countess to appear before him. She fails to appear at the designated time and is summoned three more times, but without effect. The king again sends for his counsellors, who are of one opinion: "that the count with his kin, with his men, and with his force should take her"[27] and punish her. When after a lengthy private war the count finally captures his aunt, she pleads for her life, pointing out that "the king has the forfeiture of my body and all my land."[28] Although the count already has permission to put his aunt to death,[29] he does not wish to forfeit her lands by a rash act; consequently he sends to the royal court a messenger who, after reviewing the history of the case before the king and "his great counsel assembled and his great barons all together,"[30] requests that the judgment and punishment of the wicked countess be committed to her nephew. The barons all consent, together with the king, who "gives him the forfeiture, for he is the rightful heir."[31] Thus with royal sanction the count and his men hold court to determine the manner in which the wicked countess shall die. Her punishment is death by fire.[32]

While this episode illustrating the relations between two different jurisdictions speaks for itself, there still remain a few comments to be made. Although the right to carry on private warfare was in existence as late as 1316,[33] it is obvious that there were some restrictions, else the Count of Bourges need not have secured the *accort du roy*. Moreover, the nature of these restrictions is suggested in the count's doubt about the right to war against his aunt, for Beaumanoir says:

the king . . . can constrain the parties to make peace or give truce; . . . and in the same way, when war takes place between those of the same lineage, the seignior [in *Comte d'Anjou* the king] must make every effort to stop the war, for otherwise the lineage may be destroyed because each in the war would be on the side of his nearest kin, whence it happens that at the same time one cousin kills another.[34]

The count, not wishing to get into trouble or to lose any property, does the wise thing by getting the king to summon his aunt; and the full significance of his maneuver becomes clear if we may temporarily apply to royal justice what Beaumanoir says of the summons for criminal cases in the county of Clermont, for according to him,

it is necessary for the summoned to come at his summons, or he will be in default. For after summons is made . . . the parties may not delay without the consent of the seignior [in *Comte d'Anjou* the king]. But it is necessary that he who has caused the summons to be made prosecute the case for which he has caused the accused to be summoned. . . . And if he prosecutes him and the accused fails to appear, the latter shall be judged for the defaults; and if there are three of them he is attainted of the matter for which he was summoned.[35]

It is not strange, then, that upon her fourth default the king's counsellors regard the wicked countess as guilty and authorize her nephew to take her by force and punish her. When she points out that the king has forfeiture of her land, she is only repeating a well-known feudal principle. Although the Count of Bourges is her heir, he cannot legally receive his aunt's fief directly, for on the death of a landholder, the legal heir generally received the fief, but only from the hands of the deceased's overlord;[36] it remained the latter's privilege to withhold the fief if he saw fit. Hence when the king gives the count forfeiture of his aunt's lands, he promises to enfeoff him of those lands when the aunt is dead. But as a matter of fact he need not wait that long, for by her defiance the countess has already lost her fief. In the actual judgment of the wicked aunt it is interesting to note that the count and all his men, together with the Duke of Brittany, who has assisted him in the war, appear to act as judges, no maximum being stipulated in actual law. There seems to be one irregularity, however, for, after hearing the opinions of the assembly, the count himself determines, with general consent, of course, the manner of death his aunt shall die, whereas in the thirteenth century and later, as president of the court, he should take no part in the deliberations but merely perform the judges' will.[37]

In the last few pages we have tried to show first, that in the romances the ecclesiastical court has no place[38] and that the justice of the royal and seignorial courts predominates; second, to illustrate from the romances the organization of these latter courts and the manner in which they function; and third, to illustrate the relations between the two and the limitations restricting the jurisdictions of each. In this attempt it has been impossible to avoid altogether some phases of procedure, particularly in the discussion of the *Comte d'Anjou.* But since the crimes committed by the wicked aunt and by Nogant in *Durmart* are at least treason if not lese majesty, it may be worth-while to investigate the nature of treason in the romances before we go on to procedure itself.

Treason

Since as already indicated, there will be no exhaustive catalog, it appears that the most interesting way in which to become acquainted with the wide variety of crime in the romances is to determine as nearly as possible what misdeeds the poets regard as treason and to determine how close the romance writers' conception approximates the actual conception of treason. In performing this task we shall find it best to discuss, first, those offenses most closely resembling lese majesty, next, those resembling the *défi féodal* or *foi mentie,* and then to proceed in due order from undeniable to more doubtful cases of treason.

As pointed out in the preceding chapter, lese majesty is neither mentioned nor defined in any of the French custumals before 1300; nor is it mentioned in any of the romances, although they furnish many instances of injury to royalty, most of which, however, involve personal hatred or secret treachery and hence fall more readily under the heading of treason than of lese majesty. An example approaching very near to the latter crime occurs in the romance *Sone de Nansai,* written probably during the latter part of the thirteenth century—a time when the seeds of the doctrine of lese majesty had already taken root. The episode is as follows:

Henri, son and deputy of Emperor Sone, is called to Sicily because the grand bailiff "has betrayed the people"[39] by cheating them out of two galleys full of fine gold and good silver which he had improperly collected on the feigned authority of the emperor's seal. When called upon to surrender the seal of his office, the bailiff answers by striking Henri upon the head with a heavy stick. Henri retaliates in kind, and the bailiff's two eyes fly out of their sockets as he falls dead from the violence of the blow.[40]

The grand bailiff has in the first place abused his power by betraying the people; next, he has not only disobeyed an imperial order, but he has also offered violence to an imperial officer, the emperor's son. The last two offenses taken together—namely, offenses against the sovereign power of the king[41]—constitute a crime fundamentally the same as the lese majesty described in the theory elaborated at the end of the fourteenth century. Although this crime is seldom mentioned even in the French legal treatises before the second half of the fourteenth century, one identical with it in everything except name is clearly indicated in *Sone de Nansai,* particularly by Henri's desire to render justice[42] as an imperial officer and by what is to be discussed later—the quartering of the bailiff's corpse. According to Perrot, numerous charters as early as the twelfth and even the eleventh century make express concessions to certain high justiciars with regard to punishment resulting from delicts committed against the king.[43]

Another offense possibly resembling lese majesty, but one which the author of the *Roman de la violette* calls merely treason, is that of truce-breaking. The hero, Girart, personally avenges the injury done to a knight, who tells him that a traitor, the treacherous Sire de Durlus, has attacked and wounded him and carried off the bride whom he has that very day espoused. The gravity of Durlus's crime becomes more apparent when we learn that, though he is admittedly the wounded knight's mortal enemy, he is himself not only an officer of the law, the justiciar of Ardene, but has also given truce to the man he betrays.[44] While Durlus's act affects immediately the injured knight and his bride, it probably also indirectly concerns the king, especially if we can suppose Durlus to have sworn the truce before a royal officer. Gerbert wrote the *Violette* about 1228,[45] only a few years after the death of Philip Augustus, during whose reign, according to Beaumanoir, royalty had instituted the *quarantaine-le-roi* and had made more precise the regulations governing the *asseurement,* thus making the violation of truce not only an offense against royalty but also the *grant traison* spoken of in the *Établissements de Saint Louis* and in the *Coutumes de Beauvaisis.*[46]

A situation that develops almost into a case of *défi féodal,* an example of the purely feudal notion of the breach of pledged faith, occurs in the romance called *Meraugis de Portlesquez:*

Belchis li Lois detains the heroine, Lidoine, against her will at his castle since he has heard that her lover, Meraugis, is dead. The still living but gravely wounded Meraugis is brought to Belchis's castle, where he recovers but keeps his identity secret. In the meantime Gawain, having heard of Lidoine's plight, comes with an army to rescue her. Meraugis, donning white armor, goes out and jousts with Gawain, to whom he makes himself known. By arrangement Gawain renders himself prisoner and is led to the castle, to the great joy of Belchis. Although Belchis wishes to put Gawain in prison, Meraugis persuades him that to do so will be unnecessary if Gawain swears fealty to him, the white knight. Belchis is so pleased by the white knight's success that, when Gawain has sworn, he himself takes the oath of fealty to Meraugis and makes his men do likewise.[47] Shortly afterward the two lovers meet, recognize, and kiss each other, much to the astonishment of Belchis, who, forgetting himself and his recent oath of fealty, shouts in anger, "You shall die! Take him!"[48]

Striving to recall Belchis to his senses, Meraugis retorts: "You take me! But I take you. Are you not my man?"[49] When the stubborn Belchis denies it, Meraugis says, "Then I accuse you of treason!"[50]

Belchis calls his men to arms, and bloodshed is imminent when Melianz de Liz, Belchis's brother-in-law, who has previously protested against swearing fealty to Meraugis, now speaks up: "Belchis, you are a fool; there are very few of yours here against him if they are not traitors. Let those know well who do amiss to my lord, whose man I am, that my force is with him against you if a fight occurs. You yourself in your court made me swear the oath; know certainly that I shall keep it."[51]

Belchis, seeing the odds against him so great, retracts his denial of fidelity and renders the lady to Meraugis.[52]

The foregoing episode gives a fairly accurate presentation of feudal relations in the twelfth and thirteenth centuries and shows the seriousness of the broken contract. In the first place, it was not unusual for a man to place himself under the protection of someone he thought more powerful than himself, as does Belchis.[53] The oath taken by Gawain, however, though imitated by Belchis and though resembling the feudal form prescribed by the *Summa de legibus* of Normandy,[54] is perhaps the oath of a particular kind of homage known as *homagium pacis,* the purpose of which was to keep peace between enemies, but which did not involve the transfer of land.[55] Nevertheless, Belchis's denial of his oath to Meraugis and his threat of personal violence do consitute the elements of the *défi féodal,* though they are not technically so called in the romance, which speaks of them in a broader sense rather as treason. Furthermore, that the threatened breach of contract between Belchis and Meraugis concerns a strictly feudal relationship, not merely personal, is shown in the settlement agreed upon by both parties. Meraugis receives the damsel, but magnanimously leaves Belchis his land,[56] which, as we already know, might legally have been forfeit. The seriousness of the breach of feudal contract is made plain in the attitude of Melianz and in that of the retainers in general, who would have regarded themselves perjured had they taken up arms against Meraugis.[57]

Having illustrated lese majesty and the *défi féodal* in the romances, and having made clear the differences between them, we may now compare treason in the romances with treason as it is defined in the custumals. Of the several crimes included in the legal definitions the most serious is murder, which the *Jostice et de plet* describes as "treason and homicide mixed together,"[58] and which, to distinguish it from simple homicide, Beaumanoir defines as the killing of a person in ambush, between sunset and sunrise, or during a truce.[59] The *Établissements de Saint Louis* adds to the details: the crime may be committed in the forest, on the highway, or while the victim is asleep in bed[60]—always, apparently, with premeditation in an atmosphere of secrecy and treachery and without warning or challenge. Murder is a theme that the romances use with many variations. It will suffice to mention only a few of them. In *Floriant et Florete* the wicked seneschal, Maragoz, rebuffed by the queen, in "vilainne traison"[61] decides to get his rival out of the way. During a hunting party Maragoz secretly puts on armor, murders the unprotected king in a desolate part of the forest, hurries back to his hiding place, takes off the armor, and returns to the main body of huntsmen in time to lament ostentatiously, like a veritable Macbeth, before the astonished nobles.[62] A more dastardly murder occurs in *Violette* when Meliatir, chagrined and goaded to desperation at having three or four teeth kicked out by Euriaut, to whom he has been unfortunate enough to make indelicate advances, resolves to avenge himself. Having concealed himself in the chamber where lie Euriaut and Ysmaine, sister of the Duke of Metz, in the dead of night Meliatir, "li trahitres,"[63] stabs Ysmaine, thinking her to be his intended victim, and places the hand of the sleeping Euriaut upon the hilt of the bloody dagger still protruding from the breast of the murdered Ysmaine.[64] But as we shall see, the criminal receives his just deserts. A similarly odious form of murder and therefore treason is attempted in the romance *Yder* when the jealous Kay, "li fels traïtres,"[65] almost succeeds in accomplishing the death of Yder by giving him water from a poisoned well to drink. Kay suffers no punishment for the crime because Yder is saved by the quick action of two passers-by who discover a faint spark of life in him.[66]

The *aguet-apensé,* the premeditated lying in wait or in ambush, which often but not always resulted in murder, was an equally serious form of treason frequently appearing in the romances. When in the romance *Yder* Kay, again "le trahitor"[67] and motivated as usual by jealousy, rushes upon Yder from the rear and thrusts a spear through his back, he is guilty of treason, which is somewhat mitigated, however, since the crime takes place before many witnesses and is therefore not the *aguet-apensé* proper. But the fact that the blow is delivered from the rear without warning or challenge makes the offense a form of treason much more serious than an attempt at simple homicide. Fortunately for Kay, Yder survives the wound, and Kay again goes unpunished. The romances offer several instances of the actual *aguet-apensé.* In *Claris et Laris,* after the two heroes in defending themselves and Laris's sister, Lydaine, have killed their wicked host, the latter's mother, through "grant mesprison . . . et grant traison,"[68] next morning seeks revenge by leading the three into an ambush of nine men, whom Claris and Laris finally overcome, only to find that in the meantime the old hag has herself attacked Lydaine, whom Claris rescues. A similar instance occurs also in the same romance: a dwarf by "sa traison"[69] leads the two unsuspecting heroes to a castle where seven robbers attack them but who are ultimately subdued. Likewise in *Claris et Laris* two brothers who for a long time have threatened a third man find him unarmed in the woods: "There they killed him disloyally, for traitors are disloyal and toward all good men are false."[70] There is no difference between this unfortunate incident and the Maragoz episode in *Floriant et Florete;* both are murder in ambush. In *Blancandin* the hero, like Girart in *Violette,* personally avenges a mortally wounded knight, who says that his enemy has

"the other day killed my father and then afterwards both my brothers; and he has cut off both my flesh and my hide, and so much done to me that I am dying. From the wounds my breath leaps from me. And with him he took my *amie*. The dishonor to her is more displeasing to me than my own hurt. He was concealed in a thicket; and he struck me in treason so that I did not see him coming at all."[71]

The similarity between the dying knight's last sentence and the first sentence of the definition of treason given in the *Jostice et de plet* is indeed noteworthy. The only technical difference between the tragedy just related and the Durlus episode in *Violette* is that Durlus has sworn to keep a truce. That all of these illustrations are examples of the *aguet-apensé* and hence treason needs no further verification.

In thirteenth century France brigandage or highway robbery was regarded as a form of treason because of its similarity to the *aguet-apensé*. Concerning this Beaumanoir says:

The second case in which Holy Church does not guarantee him who is guilty, is of him who is a highway robber in ambush; for when he is pursued for such a deed and he flees for protection to a sanctuary, the place does not guarantee that justice cannot take him and judge him as a thief and traitor.[72]

According to the romances the purpose of brigandage was to gain valuable posessions, such as armor and fine horses. The romance *Durmart* provides an excellent example of the medieval robber-baron and horse thief in "li fel trahitres desloialz,"[73] Fel de la Garde, who later reforms and becomes an exemplary member of the Round Table. A clear line of demarcation should be drawn between treason and petty thievery. One incident in *Fergus* illustrates both offenses. Fergus, hungry from a two-day fast, joins a party of fifteen robber knights who are roasting chickens over a fire. Since chicken-stealing is not treason, these men are up to this point merely thieves; they become traitors, however, when after the meal they attack Fergus without warnning. He kills all but two, whom he sends to Arthur's court.[74] The trouble with the average medieval robber was that, like a certain scoundrel described by the author of *Richars li biaus,* he was "non mie lerez, mais mourdreres,"[75] and consequently in most cases guilty of treason.

Having clearly indicated the status of murder, ambush, and brigandage as recognized forms of treason in the romances, and having verified them as such by reference to the actual laws of thirteenth century France, we may now profitably inquire into the less obvious forms of treason and into the "many similar cases" that Beaumanoir includes in his definition, our purpose being to ascertain whether the romances are generally correct in applying as widely as they do the term *treason.* Beaumanoir himself in his chapter on *tricherie,* the definition of which is quoted in Chapter II under the heading of treason, suggests standards for determining what these "similar cases" may be:

And if an evil deed has occurred through *tricherie,* for which the doers should receive death, he by whose *tricherie* this [particular evil deed] was done ought to bear a penalty similar to that of those who did it, for there is little difference between the *tricheeur* and traitor. For the *tricheeur* often wishes to cover his *tricherie* by fair words, and it often happens that he accomplishes it [*tricherie*] so treacherously and so slyly that one cannot obtain witnesses against him.[76]

Obviously, then, the many "similar cases" included such crimes as forgery and false accusation, which indeed might be regarded as treason, depending upon the degree of harm done or even intended. It may therefore be reasoned that any treachery or deception not only possibly resulting in death or serious harm to the victim but also possibly resulting in the infliction upon the criminal of the usual punishment given a traitor might well be regarded as treason, especially since there is little difference between the *tricheeur* and the traitor. With this guide to Beaumanoir's "many other similar cases" we may now further explore the romances for examples of treason not already clearly recognized as such.

Although one may hunt in vain through the *Coutumes de Beauvaisis* for any mention of forgery as treason, one will be rewarded by turning to Beaumanoir's romance, *La Manekine,* in which the wicked mother-in-law, motivated partly by hatred, attempts through forgery "qui par traïson fu letree"[77] to have her son's wife and child burned at the stake. Though her purpose is frustrated by the kindness of the seneschal (who sets mother and child adrift in a boat instead of burning them), Beaumanoir nevertheless speaks of the mother-in-law's crime as "le murdre et la grant traïson,"[78] not only because murder and treason would have resulted had her will been accomplished, but because, though her attempt has failed, her hatred and malice, the first conditions of treason, are clearly evident. In the *Comte d'Anjou* a similar forgery is likewise justifiably called "traïson desloiaus."[79] In *Sone de Nansai,* however, there is an instance of forgery whose status as treason is not at once so clearly established. Godefroi de Mesnil, who has signed a note for two thousand *livres,* is ruined by the royal bailiff, who forges the note to read one hundred thousand *livres* and who has dispossessed many a baron in similar fashion. While the bailiff is called "traytor de put 'aire,"[80] he is also spoken of as "chilz grans leres baillieus souvrains."[81] Obviously the bailiff is guilty of deception and treachery, and while he is a traitor in the sense that he has misused his office, he is perhaps as much thief as traitor, according to Beaumanoir, who says: "But where such fraud can be detected, the cheaters who commit the fraud and all consenting to it ought to be punished as thieves."[82] Yet there is no reason why this particular thief should not be punished also as a traitor, for his purpose is to dispossess Godefroi, and

Beaumanoir says that to bear false testimony in order to dispossess a man is treason.

False accusation, a form of malicious treachery and hence potentially treason, occurs with variations throughout the romances. In *Durmart* the vassal-king Nogant, twitted with cowardice, makes war upon his cousin and feudal superior, Queen Fenise of Ireland. When Durmart comes to her aid, Nogant, "comme fel trahitres proves,"[83] in order to offset the disadvantage, sends for help to King Arthur, asserting, as we already know, that Fenise is a heretic and that therefore she is usurping his rightful place. Such treachery as this, if not lese majesty, is undoubtedly treason, for it is bearing false testimony in order to dispossess; moreover, if convicted of heresy, Fenise would have not only to forfeit her kingdom and property but in addition would have to suffer death by fire.

The accusation of heresy, however, was not as popular among traitors as that of adultery. In the romance *Joufrois* the wicked seneschal thus "con traites"[84] falsely accuses the queen, who has discouraged his protestations of love. Here the treachery amounts to treason, for through the seneschal's hatred and malice, the king, believing the charge, is with difficulty persuaded to refrain from hanging or burning Queen Halis before the claim is proved invalid by due process of law. The accusation remains the same in several other romances, but the details vary. In the Middle English romance, *The Erle of Toulouse,* two nobles whose love the queen has rejected persuade a young and unsuspecting knight to conceal himself in the queen's room. When she has gone to bed, the two nobles, raising a hue and cry, rush in, slay the young knight, and accuse the queen of adultery before the hastily assembled barons.[85] Again, no matter what fate might be in store for the queen, this deception is obviously treason not only because of the wanton killing that has been committed, but also because it constitutes the bearing of false testimony in order to have a person put to death.

The imputation of adultery takes a new turn in the *Comte de Poitiers,* in which a discussion of the Countess of Poitiers's virtue leads to a wager between the Duke of Normandy and the count to the effect that should the former seduce the countess, the latter loses his lands to the winner. The Duke of Normandy, "le traïtor,"[86] fails utterly in his purpose, but in order not to lose the wager, he enlists the aid of the wicked nurse Alotru, who procures for him certain of the countess's intimate possessions, which he produces in Pepin's court as evidence of his conquest. According to Beaumanoir, such chicanery is indeed treason, for through his falsehood the duke dispossesses the count. Moreover, while there is no formal accusation of adultery, the claim pressed by the duke is equivalent to one. His offense, therefore, together with that of Alotru, may further be regarded as treason since the countess's life is jeopardized by the count's intention of killing her—a right perhaps not yet completely suppressed in the first quarter of the thirteenth century—the approximate date of the romance—which was some years before Beaumanoir recorded the restriction prohibiting husbands from killing their wives except if they found them specifically in the act of adultery.[87]

Almost the identical situation occurs in *Violette* when Girart wagers his lands that his sweetheart, Euriaut, cannot be seduced by Lisiart. Like the Duke of Normandy, "li trechiere"[88] Lisiart fails completely, but through the connivance of the old nurse Gondree, he obtains a sight of Euriaut in her bath and observes a mark resembling a violet under her right breast. He returns to court boasting of his conquest, proof of which he gives in the mention of Euriaut's curious birthmark. Lisiart's deception, while unquestionably treason in that it dispossesses Girart, may have been treason on a second count, but not according to thirteenth century law: Beaumanoir not only says nothing about the right of the betrothed man to take the life of the betrothed though unfaithful woman, but even denies to any man the right to slay his daughter, sister, niece, or ward, guilty of fornication[89]—a right which some early Germanic customs granted to the father of an unchaste daughter and also to the brother of an erring sister, especially if the brother acted as head of the family.[90] But since Girart leads Euriaut into the forest to take her life, he may have been acting upon a custom similar to the old Burgundian law which stipulated the death penalty for the betrothed woman who espoused another man.[91] If not according to the thirteenth century law, then perhaps only according to Burgundian law or to the literary demands of the romance itself does the deception of Lisiart endanger the life of Euriaut and therefore constitute the crime of treason on the second count.

As in *Violette,* the heroine of Jehan Renart's romance of *Guillaume de Dole* is implicated, through deception, in a claim of unchastity. Emperor Conrad, having heard of Lienor's beauty, sends for her brother Guillaume, gives him royal welcome and high favor, and informs him of his desire to wed Lienor. A seneschal at court, jealous of Guillaume's favor with the emperor, seeks to avenge himself by disgracing Lienor. Like Lisiart and the Duke of Normandy, he goes to the home of the lady, but is not allowed to see her in the absence of her brother. The seneschal's bestowal of rich gifts upon the mother, however, loosens her tongue and she speaks proudly of her daughter, thoughtlessly mentioning the rose-like mark on Lienor's thigh. The wicked seneschal—never has any man conceived such "traïson mortel"[92]—returns to court and advises Conrad not to marry Lienor because he says she has formerly been his mistress; he mentions the mark of the rose to verify his statement. Here again, according to thirteenth century law, the seneschal's treachery may not be treason, for theoretically Lienor's life cannot be jeopardized since Beaumanoir says nothing of the brother's right over the life of his unchaste sister. But in the romance, Guillaume, hearing the seneschal's story from the emperor, sends his nephew to wreak vengeance upon Lienor. Actually her life is in danger, for the nephew assures Guillaume, "I shall kill her with my two hands."[93] Thus in a sense the seneschal is guilty of treason. But there is another side to the seneschal's treachery which may possibly reveal him as "traitres lerres murtriers,"[94] for his whole scheme has been to regain the emperor's favor by discrediting his rival, and Beaumanoir tells us that, among other things, to make one hated of one's liege lord is treason. As revealed later, the seneschal is duly punished for his treason.

One wonders whether, in view of all these accusations of adultery and unchastity, such misdeeds as adultery and rape themselves were not treason. Although adultery—a crime which not only threatened the foundations of heredity and parental responsibility,[95] but which also set in operation the law of vengeance—was considered treason in early times,[96] it is doubtful, because of changing social conditions, whether in the twelfth and thirteenth centuries it was universally so regarded, especially since in the thirteenth century it generally came under the jurisdiction of the ecclesiastical courts. None of the custumals speaks of adultery as treason, and while it occurs in the romances, Chrétien de Troyes is perhaps the only poet to suggest that it is treason;[97] in fact, according to the romance called *Châtelain de Coucy,* it is treason to inform the cuckolded husband of his wife's illicit liaison.[98] On the other hand, the abduction or the forcing of a woman, married or single, against her will, was a frequent occurrence, if we may interpret Beaumanoir literally,[99] and was moreover definitely called treason in the romances. In *Cléomadès,* when Crompart flies off with the beautiful Clarmondine on the wooden horse, the golden trumpeter blows his horn to announcé treason.[100] In *Claris et Laris,* after Mordres has unsuccessfully attempted to force a damsel, no less a person that Gawain rescues him from an impromptu hanging by the lady's two avenging brothers and soundly rates him for his conduct as follows:

"Brother," says he, "a gentleman of great rank truly commits too great an outrage who forces a woman . . . for it is a very great misprision and cruelty and treason, for a woman cannot defend herself, since by nature she is soft and tender, and a man bold and rough and strong."[101]

Like adultery, this crime, involving insult to the family honor and thus bringing about the deadly feud, may have been considered a form of treason in early times; it was not, however, so spoken of in thirteenth century customary law, which nevertheless grouped it together with murder, treason, and homicide—all cases of high justice. That the forcing of a woman was popularly, however, if not legally, thought of as treason is shown in at least one official record, for according to the *Registre criminel de Saint-Germain-des-Prés* (16 decembre 1280, 3 février 1281), a certain Baudoin accused of treason ("apelet de traison") and termed a false traitor ("faus traitoir") one Rendoul, who had forcibly lain with Baudoin's wife.[102]

With the one or two minor exceptions already noted, we may safely conclude that treason in the romances differs little, either in concept or in form, from treason in the actual law and custom of twelfth and thirteenth century France.

Procedure

Had the Baudoin just referred to lived in Merovingian times, it is probable that instead of appealing to the courts he would have taken the law into his own hands. We may here find it appropriate, therefore, to begin the account of procedure by describing one of its earlier phases as appearing in the romances—namely, that phase which developed from the law of vengeance at a time when the offended party or his representative was the executer of the death penalty and when the offender's corpse or head was exposed in a conspicuous place in order to advertise the fact that his execution was entirely legal as the consequence of crime committed. Very likely it is some form of this defensive measure of procedure which impels a damsel in *Claris et Laris* to attach the head of her lover's murderer, put to death by the knight Gales, to the tail of her horse and drag it to her castle, where she has it hung from a gibbet.[103] It is perhaps a similar motive which causes Gaheriez, in the same romance, to hang from the branches of two trees the corpses of a couple of thieves whom he has found in flagrant delinquency and whom he has therefore lawfully put to the sword.[104] In the somewhat extravagant romance *Fergus,* the hero, attacked by four robbers at a crossroads, puts two to flight and kills two, whose heads he cuts off and attaches by their beards to his saddle.[105] Proceeding then to court, where Kay jokes prolixly at his expense, the rustic Fergus, in the act of asking permission to go on a fantastic quest, is interrupted by Arthur, who has shown perhaps too much patience throughout Kay's tediousness. "Tell me, if it does not annoy you," interposes the courteous monarch, "where you took these two heads. . . ."[106] One wonders whether exaggerated politeness or judicial laxity has atrophied Arthur's rightful curiosity when he says casually, "if it does not annoy you," for though the heads are in a sense evidence that Fergus has only exercised his proper legal rights, curious authorities in Merovingian times were neither casual nor reticent about making further investigation. Gregory of Tours says that one Chramnisund, who, insulted by a man named Sichar, had killed the latter, "stripped the body of its garments, hung it from a post of his fence, and ridden away to the king," was sentenced by the king "to prove that he had slain Sichar for his honor."[107] Although the bodies or the dissevered members of criminals were still publicly exposed in the twelfth and thirteenth centuries, this barbaric form of procedure had no doubt become more a feature of public than of private justice.

During these centuries legal procedure assumed a rigid formality generally reflected throughout the romances under discussion and appearing to best advantage in the strictness by which the court held persons involved in civil or criminal processes closely to the words they uttered. In speaking of the word-for-word formality Brunner cites[108] two instances from Chrétien's *Yvain* which admirably illustrate the pitfalls endangering the legal path of the rash or the ignorant. When Yvain and Lancelot have ceased their combat over the claims of the disinherited damsel and her cruel sister, King Arthur (still the gracious monarch, but here more businesslike than in *Fergus*), seeing that justice has not been advanced by force of arms and wishing to settle the matter conclusively, trips the older sister by means of a neatly put question:

"Where is the damsel," he inquires, "who has ejected her sister from her land and has forcibly and cruelly disinherited her?"

"My lord," she answers, "here I am."

"Are you there? Then draw near to me! I saw plainly some time ago that you were disinheriting her. But her right shall no longer be denied; for you yourself have avowed the truth to me. You must now resign her share to her."

"Sire," says she, "if I uttered a foolish and thoughtless word, you ought not to take me up in it."[109]

Earlier in the same romance Lunete explains her predicament to Yvain as follows:

In full court and in the presence of all he [Laudine's seneschal] accused me of having betrayed her in your favor. And I had no counsel or aid except my own; but I knew that I had never done or conceived any treacherous act towards my lady, so I cried out, as one beside herself, and without the advice of anyone that I would present in my own defense one knight who should fight against three.[110] The fellow was not courteous enough to scorn to accept such odds, nor was I at liberty to retreat or withdraw for anything that might happen. So he took me at my word. . . .[111]

Although the perils of speaking in court without advice from counsel are manifest, in the romances under discussion counsellors as individual members of the species appear rarely, and never under the name *avocat;*[112] generally they are more gregarious in their habits, like the king's counsellors and the count's advisers in the *Comte d'Anjou,* who when required act also as judges. A practically isolated and somewhat dubious example of the individual counsellor occurs in the romance *Rigomer.* Lancelot, whom Chrétien describes as "well acquainted with suits and laws, trials and verdicts,"[113] here first offers unsuccessfully to serve as legal adviser and later combats successfully for a widow deprived of her dowry by her former husband's nephew.[114] It must be said in all fairness to Lancelot, however, that his failure to act as counsel is really the fault of the widow, who in court, like Lunete, had said things that she was not permitted to retract. Lancelot's legal conference with the widow consists merely in his finding out whether her case is *bona fide* in order that his oath before battle may not be a perjured one.[115]

In the criminal procedure of the romances the proof, whether it be flagrant delinquency, presumption, compurgation, or one of the judgments of God, presents a most interesting and fruitful subject for treatment, not only representing the age but at the same time offering material dear to the heart of the narrative poet. Thus the account of these dramatic methods of proof in the romances may be begun in no better way than by the discussion of flagrant delinquency in the *Erle of Toulouse*, the *Châtelain de Coucy*, and *Violette*.

We are already familiar with the situation in the *Erle of Toulouse*, which accounts for one reason why the proof by witness had fallen into disrepute in the feudal period and at the same time shows that to be caught in the act was not always the best proof of one's guilt. In the poem the two rejected admirers of Dame Beulybon have rushed into her chamber after she has retired, killed the young Sir Antore concealed there at their instigation, and have accused the queen of adultery before the assembled barons. Proof of her guilt they offer in the corpse of young Antore, found in the deed, they themselves acting as avenging witnesses. The unfortunate part is that in the following trial the nobles in their parliament can find no law to save the queen from death. The success of the traitors seems assured until one old knight, smelling a rat, speaks up. He points out that no one has ever found any villainy in the queen save the two accusers; furthermore, the same two have slain Antore without permitting him to utter a word in self-defense. The old knight, suspecting that "Be some hateryd hyt may be,"[116] suggests a combat to decide the question of the queen's guilt—a guilt which before he speaks has apparently been self-evident. Although not mentioned in the romance, there is another reason why the action of the traitors is open to question: while the law permits the husband to kill the adulterous wife and her lover if found in the deed, it says nothing whatever of any person's right to put to death the wife of another man *or her lover*.[117]

In contrast to the preceding the *Châtelain de Coucy*

illustrates the great restraint exercised by the lord of Fayel, whose wife carries on a secret and adulterous amour:

Having been informed of his wife's infidelity with the Châtelain de Coucy, the Sire de Fayel, completely armed[118] and with his man Gobert as helper and witness, slips by night inside the garden gate in order to catch the lovers in flagrant delinquency. The lady of Fayel, slightly indisposed, has not left her room, but Isabel, the confidante, on hearing the gate, goes to meet one who is, she thinks, the châtelain. She is frightened first at seeing Fayel and then a moment later the châtelain himself. Fayel accuses the châtelain, who denies the implication of adultery, saying that he has come only to see Isabel; she bears him out in this assertion. In the meantime, Gobert having informed the lady of Fayel that "my lord wishes to kill him [the châtelain],"[119] she pretends to fear robbers and thus further disconcerts the husband, who is finally persuaded to let the châtelain go in peace.

That Fayel's purpose is violent revenge is clear from the fact that he goes to the garden fully armed and intending to kill. But unlike the accusers in the *Erle of Toulouse,* he allows the châtelain to speak in self-defense, particularly since he has not previously forbidden the châtelain to enter the premises and since by chance his wife is not present and he does not catch the lovers in the act, as he has expected to do. Fayel seems fully aware of Beaumanoir's restriction of the husband's right. Furthermore, since he is a seignior and probably holds court himself, or at least acts as an *echevin*—for he has once told the châtelain that he was going "à un plait"[120]—he doubtless realizes not only that his evidence is not clear, but also that his own life is legally forfeit if he kills a man not actually in flagrant delinquency.[121]

In *Violette,* when Euriaut is found with her hand on the hilt of the bloody dagger with which Meliatir has murdered Ysmaine, the situation is somewhat different from those in the two preceding illustrations, in the first of which, witnesses have ostensibly discovered the criminal in the act. In *Violette,* however, there is no witness, but the complaint is the same: that the offender has been found in the deed. While Euriaut is at the stake ready to be burnt, her lover, Girart, appears on the scene and offers to combat for her, but is insultingly informed by her accuser, Meliatir, that since she has been found in the deed, the evidence is too clear to admit any other proof. The Duke of Metz, silencing the growing quarrel, says, "I wish to judge her fairly; without trial I do not wish to execute her."[122] At his request twelve peers then step aside to take counsel, agreeing to hear the opinions of two of their number and to abide by the better one. Sire de Lansi, Meliatir's kinsman, urges Euriaut's death while Sire d'Aspremont, who knows more of pleas and laws than any other knight in the world, speaks in defense of the lady. The debate is well worth reproducing in full, for Sire de Lansi's argument is not only representative of the type used in the accusatory system, but Sire d'Aspremont's defense is so much shrewder that though he does not really expose the fallacy in his opponent's argument—namely, that Euriaut is found after the fact and not in the deed—he does appear considerably more practical and suggests, perhaps without realizing it, that the basic question of the debate arises from the confusion existing between two methods of proof, flagrant delinquency and presumption. Sire de Lansi, leaning easily upon his baton, begins:

"Lords, now listen. She who was found doing the deed was in so far proved caught [in the act] that she was still holding the knife with which she had killed the damsel; moreover, such is the testimony that she had the knife in the body [of her victim] in such manner that she was holding the handle; and who would not give it as his opinion, since she was found in such guise, that she had killed her? The fact and the sight [circumstantial evidence] prove that for him who is found in such a plight, there is neither battle nor law. With these words I avow that one ought by lawful judgment to burn and deliver her to suffering. . . ."[123] [When Sire de Lansi has thus rested his case, Sire d'Aspremont rises to reply:] "Lords, now hear, listen to me a little. The man who undertakes judgment does evil when he undertakes it, since it is a sin to say wrong or condemn anyone to death if one does not know a true reason for it. Indeed you have heard the judgment that Sire de Lansi gave, that she was found thus: that she was still holding the knife that Ysmaine had in her breast, plunged in up to the handle. I say, such is my opinion, that if she had struck her, she would have fled immediately. Do you think she would go to sleep there? Certainly, never would she undertake so bold an act; one may be sure that if she had done so, she would immediately have gone away; but she was found sleeping. Know, this is proved truth, that she did not strike her in her sleep; and I know well, I do not doubt at all, if she had struck her while awake, I should wonder very much if she had not fled at once. In accordance with the law, and [by this] I mean justice, let someone go to her and ask her whether she has done this murder or not. If she says no, let Meliatir, whom I just now heard give challenge, take shield and lance, for she already has her champion. And so let me avow that this undertaking had better be put upon him, I think; and may God acquit the damsel if she be not culpable."[124]

The whole debate is an interesting if not very logical one. Sire de Lansi offers a proof by presumption and thinks he has demonstrated the suspects caught in the act. Sire d'Aspremont merely explodes one presumption by another, which, we must grant, is more plausible than the first, not only because it is more reasonable but because it is probably based on the law of flight, which states that if a suspect held in prison escapes and flees, the act of flight proves him guilty of the crime he is suspected of.[125] It is easy to see how the converse, the fact that Euriaut has not attempted flight after supposedly committing a crime, has strongly impressed Sire d'Aspremont and his hearers. To them, since there is now a possibility of her innocence, the proof of flagrant delinquency is no longer tenable, and after Euriaut, yellow as beeswax from fright, has denied the charge, the question of her guilt is decided by judicial combat, in which Girart proves her innocent.[126]

Having seen that the proof of flagrant delinquency in the romances is for the most part really a form of presumption, we may now examine the latter proof in more detail since it appears particularly in the romance episodes dealing with the wager and the curious birthmark. In the *Comte de Poitiers* the Duke of Normandy has secured through the nurse Alotru as evidence of his conquest of the Countess of Poitiers her wedding ring, ten of her hairs, and a portion of sendal from one of her garments, which he produces in Pepin's court. The stolen hairs are successfully matched with the countess's golden tresses. And although she denies the Duke's assertion, appeals to her husband not to believe the traitor, and offers to undergo the judgment of boiling lead, Pepin says: "By St. Denise, no judgment will be taken. The nobles say . . . your tokens have proved you. . . . He deceived you by lechery; thus he shall have Poitiers and Normandy, and you shall have poverty and shame."[127] Hence Pepin and the nobles consider the countess guilty of adultery. The case is obviously one of clear presumption on the part of the court, which regards its presumption upon the evidence produced by the duke as equivalent to proof. That such a proof is considered incontrovertible is shown in Pepin's denying to the countess the privilege of undergoing an ordeal to manifest her innocence.

In *Violette* Lisiart, like the Duke of Normandy in the *Comte de Poitiers,* offers proof of his seduction of Euriaut in the mention of her unusual birthmark, knowledge of which he has gained through the aid of the nurse Gondree. The heroine is utterly dumbfounded at the disclosure, and suspecting treason, as does the Countess of Poitiers, says as much. But strangely enough she does not deny Lisiart's assertion, nor does she offer to prove her innocence, as does the countess. In hurt wonder she merely surmises that Lisiart could have learned of the birthmark only through her friends.[128] Such remarks, of course, carry no weight in court since they do not constitute a formal denial. And just as the Count of Poitiers believes his wife guilty of adultery, so Girart, angered at his sweetheart's utterance, believes her guilty of unchastity, for proof of her guilt is now common knowledge. Why has Euriaut failed to defend her reputaton in the eyes of the court and particularly in the eyes of her lover, who has just lost his land through her? If we remember Esmein's statement to the effect that in the accusatory system the judge is compelled to limit his investigation entirely to the evidence furnished by the accuser, and if we remember the nature of the proof of clear presumption, we shall understand that, after all, Euriaut does the best thing, for we have already seen the futility of the Countess of Poitiers's denial; moreover, it would be not merely useless but humiliating for Euriaut to protest her innocence, for should she do so, Lisiart has only to request an examination of her by matrons appointed by the court to verify his contention about the birthmark.

The perverse logic of the presumptive proof is shown perhaps to better advantage in *Guillaume de Dole* since in this romance it jeopardizes the guilty instead of the innocent. The situation is as follows:

When the wicked seneschal advises the Emperor Conrad not to marry Lienor because he says she has been his mistress and mentions the rose-like mark to verify this statement, her brother Guillaume, horrified, sends his nephew to punish her. The nephew is soon undeceived, however, and together he and Lienor set out for Mayence. Upon their arrival Lienor sends by a trusted squire a girdle, a purse, a ring, and a cloth to the seneschal as presents from the châtelaine of Dijon, who begs him to wear these gifts about his person as tokens of their mutual regard. The seneschal accepts them with surprise and pleasure. Lienor, whose identity is unknown to all except her nephew, then goes to the palace and formally accuses the seneschal not only of rape but also of robbery. The archbishop of Cologne, happening to be present, suggests a respite to determine the truth of her contention. The seneschal is searched and the stolen articles are found upon him. The evidence is so clear, the case is so apparent that no further proof, as by combat, is necessary to manifest his guilt. The seneschal, however, denies the charge, asserting that he has never seen his accuser before, and even hints that the articles have been put upon him by enchantment. He offers to undergo a judgment to prove his innocence or to get a hundred knights to swear to it. But these privileges are denied him because, since he is already proved guilty, the law can offer him no other means of redress. He then asks leave to undergo a judgment, not as a legal right, but as a favor for his past services. Even Conrad is moved to pity, but he says he can do nothing without the lady's consent. When the barons all go to her for mercy, she accords with them. The seneschal is proved innocent in a cold water judgment. Only then Lienor reveals her identity and shows that since the seneschal has never seen her before, his slanderous assertions concerning her character must necessarily be false. Guillaume is then informed of the good news, and in the evening the emperor's wedding is celebrated while the seneschal awaits his sentence in prison.[129]

The modern reader will immediately ask why, aside from the fact that the seneschal needs a good wetting for his behavior, Lienor follows such a round-about method instead of giving him the lie direct. But Lienor is far from stupid. Servois remarks that even Boccaccio's Ginevra is less clever than she is.[130] Her action, though ingenious, is as a matter of fact about the only legal course open to her if she wishes to put the seneschal in his place, and she knows it, having, as the poet tells us in no uncertain terms, studied the law for five years.[131] In the first place, Lienor apparently anticipates Beaumanoir by some eighty years through the knowledge that she cannot in her own character formally accuse the seneschal of deception or *tricherie* after what he has said of her, since a defamed person cannot legally accuse of *tricherie* another person in good repute; however, she may have been following an old capitulary of Frankish times.[132] Lienor knows, furthermore, that a straightforward denial and a protestation of her innocence would prove embarrassing because of the examination that she would be subjected to, should the seneschal request a confirmation of his statement about the birthmark. She understands perfectly that the judge must limit his investigation entirely to the evidence furnished by the accuser and accordingly proceeds to cast suspicion in the right direction by confronting the unwary seneschal with the double accusation of rape and robbery after having planted evidence of the latter upon him, realizing full well what the court's reaction is likely to be when the seneschal cannot satisfactorily explain how he has come into possession of the supposedly stolen articles.[133] The reason for the double accusation becomes plain when we understand all that is involved in Lienor's desire to prove herself innocent of unchastity. She realizes that if she accuses the seneschal of rape alone, her case is legally ruined, for upon such a charge, according to the *Très ancien coutumier de Normandie,* she would be examined by matrons of the court for signs of violence.[134] It is to avoid such an examination that she accuses the seneschal also of robbery, proof of which alone is enough to cause his execution. But Lienor wants first and foremost to show herself innocent of unchastity; consequently, she agrees with the barons to let the seneschal take the cold water test, which has particular significance here since the *Très ancien coutumier de Normandie* says that when the court is satisfied that a damsel has been violated, the man she accuses may, if he wishes, try to clear himself by just this kind of judgment.[135] Thus through a knowledge of the law Lienor has cast so much suspicion on her slanderer that she has avoided embarrassment herself and has forced the seneschal to prove himself a liar and her innocent by the form of proof befitting the occasion. Inasmuch as no one at Conrad's court knows who she is except her brother, who is ill with grief, and her nephew, who understands her purpose, she has executed her plan without hindrance, not failing to seize the golden opportunity. The success of her endeavor has, however, hinged entirely upon the presumptive proof which reveals the seneschal as a "robber" and which from the first has cast him under suspicion of the court.

The seneschal's offer, in *Guillaume de Dole,* to have one hundred knights swear to his innocence is perhaps the only suggestion in the romances under discussion of what the Middle Ages called the proof by compurgation. Almost as rare in these poems is mention of the judgments of God excepting that of battle.[136] Although Queen Fenise offers to undergo the ordeal of fire and the Countess of Poitiers that of boiling lead, neither actually performs the test. Since the above-mentioned seneschal's cold water judgment is the only ordeal actually performed, we may read the poet's brief account of it:

The court was forthwith all ready at the church of my Lord St. Peter, which was covered with ivy leaves. All came there, both prince and vassal, and the seneschal, who was brought; and the damsel came along, at the advice of the archbishop, to see true justice. With great shame because of her girdle [which Lienor had planted upon the seneschal] was the seneschal regarded. As soon as he had entered within, into the water which was consecrated, forthwith more quickly than a hatchet went all of his body to the bottom so that the fair Lienor saw that he was saved—and all the others who on the one side and on the other were gathered about the vat. The clerks praised God very much for it in their chants and in their sacred singing.[137]

The very frequency of the familiar trial by battle, however, not only makes up for the scarcity of the other tests, but renders unnecessary here a full account of judicial duels in the romances.[138] In spite of the opportunity for deceit and treachery in this dangerous form of proof,[139] most duels in the romances under discussion turn out successfully for the cause of righteousness. A good illustration, occurring in the first episode of *Joufrois,* is worth touching upon because of the detailed description of the ceremony and formality involved:

Joufroi challenges the wicked seneschal, who has falsely accused Queen Halis of adultery with a kitchen boy. The king accepts their gages and takes hostages from each, at the same time appointing a day for the combat. On the eve of battle Joufroi kneels in prayer before the altar and the crucifix. The flicker of many candles illumines the vast arches of the church. Five hundred knights, barefoot and in penitential garments, watch with the young warrior throughout the night. Before the altar of St. Mary, Queen Halis watches with well a thousand dames, likewise in penitential garb. They pray, strike themselves with blows, bow low to the ground, say orisons, give alms, read psalters, and call upon God for victory while the felon seneschal sleeps soundly all night, confident in his prowess. At the flush of dawn Joufroi hears mass at the principal altar, makes his offering of money and fine jewels, crosses himself, and calls for his arms. At the field, after the seneschal swears upon the sacred relics that the queen is an adulteress, Joufroi likewise swears upon the relics that the seneschal is a perjurer. Joufroi wins the battle.[140]

What might be called an ordeal, but an unconventional or irregular one and not a proof, occurs in the romance *Gilles de Chin.* The valet of one of Gilles's knights, seeing his master in argument with another knight, strikes the latter a hard blow. The offended one goes to the Queen of Jerusalem and demands justice, which, according to the local custom, requires the cutting off of the valet's hand.[141] Gilles, however, asks the queen's mercy for his knight's valet, but the queen, whose offers of love Gilles has previously rejected, seizes the opportunity for revenge and says she will grant mercy to the valet only on condition that Gilles himself, on horseback, leap into a pit more than twenty feet deep. In sight of all Gilles leaps into the pit, but God aiding him, neither he nor his horse is injured.[142]

Punishment

The occasional mention of punishment, though having thus far helped only to provide a better understanding of certain phases of criminal law and procedure in the romances, has given us no thorough account of a subject which we may now investigate in some detail. In doing so, we shall refer as often as possible to punishments inflicted for crimes occurring in the romances which we have already discussed in this chapter.

To begin with, one might almost say that all chastisements inflicted upon criminals in the romances are authentic since judges in real life and particularly in fiction had a certain arbitrary discretion, their only difficulty often being to decide upon one of a number of cruel punishments. Yet while most punishments in the romances correspond to those usually prescribed in the thirteenth century custumals—namely, drawing and hanging, burning, and mutilation[143]—there are occasionally some which are best explained by reference to an earlier historical period. Much more rarely, on the other hand, do the twelfth and thirteenth century romances foreshadow the legal punishments of a later day.

The late thirteenth century romance *Sone de Nansai* is almost ahead of its time in this respect, for the bailiff of Sicily, whose crime really corresponds in everything except name to the notion of lese majesty elaborated in late fourteenth century France, is finally disposed of in a manner rare in the late thirteenth century.[144] This treatment, quartering, was definitely associated with the act of lese majesty at least by the first quarter of the fourteenth century,[145] though perhaps not in France until later.[146] What happens to the bailiff after Henri has killed him by a blow of his club is set forth as follows:

Henri, who wished to render justice, caused the bailiff to be cut to pieces; in four quarters was he divided, harnessed to four horses. The one went to Trapes. One of the three which were left was sent on the road to Reggio, and the third went to Brindisi; the fourth went to Lombardy. Now had Henri apportioned the body.[147]

The form of punishment just described should not be confused with the treatment of Ganelon in the *Chanson de Roland,* which Baist regards as "most fantastic,"[148] probably because the early Germanic laws do not mention quartering,[149] though it is well established that in early times criminals were sometimes drawn apart by horses;[150] and there is little reason to suppose that people lacked sufficient ingenuity to use four horses as well as three or two. To Grimm the term *quartering* evidently connotes equine quartering, but DuCange indicates that the act might be done after the criminal has been drawn, hanged, and beheaded ("tractioni, suspendio, decollationi, . . . Quarterizationi"; "tractioni, suspensioni, . . . decapitationi et Quarternizationi");[151] moreover, though two verbs he uses (dilaniare, discindere) suggest tearing apart, possibly by horses, two other verbs (seco, disseco) suggest cleaving or cutting. And while one of the later custumals of Anjou and Maine (1437) uses the term *équartelé* in connection with lese majesty, it says nothing at all about horses.[152] We may be fairly certain, therefore, that in *Sone de Nansai* the bailiff is not drawn apart by four horses, for the text uses the word *depechier* (to cut to pieces), not the word *détraire* (to draw apart), and does not mention the animals until after the quartering has apparently been done.

Although quartering did become the conventional punishment for lese majesty, the crime of truce-breaking—a form of treason possibly resembling lese majesty, though not so closely as the breaking of the *asseurement,* which toward the end of the thirteenth century became definitely a case for royal courts only[153]—was punished in the realm of Saint Louis by hanging.[154] In Normandy a capital penalty was invoked if the truce had been sworn in a court of record, but only a simple penalty if in the hearing of a viscounty.[155] Although we have no way of knowing for certain, it is likely that the truce mentioned in the *Roman de la violette* has been sworn in as high a court as possible, higher at least than that of Durlus, justiciar of Ardene, for his victim could hardly be satisfied by anything less than the most binding of legal agreements. Should the law take its normal course, hanging, the most disgraceful of deaths, would therefore be the chastisement dealt out to Durlus for a truce-breaking which comprises not only abduction and injury but perhaps an offense against royalty as well. But in the romance, personal punishment supersedes the law of the courts, and Durlus meets his death not by hanging, but by the avenging sword of the hero Girart.[156]

Although the truce-breaking in *Violette* is irregularly punished, in *Meraugis* the *défi féodal,* the breach of purely feudal faith, goes entirely unpunished. Should Belchis commit an act of violence in addition to defying his feudal superior, however, he would not only lose the fief as punishment for the *défi féodal,* but would also very likely be drawn and hanged as a traitor for his act of violence. But by discovering before it is too late that discretion is the better part of valor, he manages to save his land as well as his life.

It is perhaps unnecessary to say that murder, a most serious form of treason, was in the thirteenth century punished by drawing and hanging. This is the manner in which Maragoz, of the romance *Floriant et Florete,* comes to his untimely end. But before we sit in at his execution, let us listen to some of the twelve kings who pass judgment upon him, for they reveal both subjective and objective aspects of the medieval philosophy of punishment and at the same time suggest a wide variety of chastisement.

Jonas, King of Tabarie, stood forth; he spoke first: "Lords," said he, "listen. True it is that Maragoz is conquered; but he was a crowned king. It is not right that he be killed: a king may not suffer death. Certainly, if we judged him, we should do great villainy; and thus I say truly indeed, no one knows what will befall him. Many a man has indeed judged another, who afterwards had shame and trouble for it since in such a deed he himself fell, and his own judgment killed him. For this reason I should say, without falsifying, that he ought to be let go."

King Brangoire came forward. "Seigniors," said he, "now listen to me. Since Maragoz is vanquished and from his mouth is the murder known, for he himself said that he killed his liege-lord, royalty may avail him nothing. In my judgment, I tell you the truth, his head must be cut off; I can find nothing else for it."

King Natalons stepped forth, who was attractive in body. "Lords," said he, "attend to me. I shall speak the truth. . . . I advise letting off King Maragoz on such condition that he shall swear forthwith that never, as long as he lives, will he enter this land."

King Bandemagus stood up, who was very well informed. "Fair lords," said he, "listen . . . Maragoz killed his seignior . . . in treason; in this he had too great misprision. For this reason I should advise, as for myself, that he be burned, faith that I owe you."

Next spoke King Turcanz, who was bold in fighting. "Lords," said he, "now attend to me. King Maragoz is vanquished and indeed confesses the treason; but to me it does not seem right, in my opinion, that he should be killed. A king must not receive death for any misbehavior that he may be able to do. Let us throw him into prison. This is the best, it is my opinion."

King Uriens rose to his feet. . . . "Seigniors," said he, "listen. According to my opinion I shall speak to you. Since Maragoz is vanquished and by a knight overcome, and since he confesses the treason, I see nothing for it but death. Now let us throw him into the sea, attach a great stone to his neck; in a little while he will be drowned; it is the best that you can do."

Next spoke King Geremie, who was lord of Hungary, "Seigniors, . . . I see no way out; so let him be hanged in the wind for it."

Lot, the rich king of Orkney, who never loved villainy, the slanderer or the deceiver, the disloyal or the traitor, now rose to his feet. "Fair lords," said he, "now hear me. Maragoz killed his lord, whereof very great disloyalty he did, and then disinherited his lady and afterwards besieged her as a traitor in Monreal; then he went to the Emperor, and caused him to come into this land. There are killed in this war full ten thousand proved knights; by him alone are all dead, for through him alone the occasion arose."[157]

The punishment that Lot goes on to suggest—namely, drawing by horse and hanging—is agreed upon by the whole court and approved by the emperor and King Arthur.

Then was Maragoz sent for, and by his two feet bound; throughout the host they dragged him, first to the rear, then forward, until he was all in pieces. Four youths, strong and lusty, came after; they took the pieces and put them all in a little mound. The king caused a gibbet to be erected; immediately, without further delay, he caused the pieces to be hanged. Thus must wicked tyrants be destroyed and brought to their end.[158]

Aside from Jonas, who in advocating no chastisement whatever seems to imply the notion that the king can do no wrong, the assembled monarchs suggest punishments which, in spite of their diversity, were inflicted generally throughout the Middle Ages for murder and treason. Brangoire, less mindful of rank than Jonas, makes his only concession to royalty in the penalty he advises, since in early times traitors in high position were sometimes beheaded instead of hanged; it will be remembered, moreover, that the sentencing of a king to death was not without parallel in history, for such a judgment, though never carried out, seems to have been imposed upon John Lackland for his supposed murder of his nephew, Arthur of Brittany.[159] Exile, suggested by King Natalons, and imprisonment, suggested by King Turcanz, often served as mitigations of the death penalty incurred for serious crimes in the Middle Ages, and particularly for that of lese majesty in the Carolingian period.[160] There is some evidence showing that Bandemagus is not altogether without precedent in advocating death by fire for Maragoz, for, though burning was often inflicted upon women in the Middle Ages, von Amira[161] notes several instances of it as a punishment for men who had committed murder. Like burning, the punishment Uriens suggests for Maragoz—namely, drowning—though often imposed upon women, was sometimes, according to von Amira, imposed upon men who were guilty of murder.[162] Finally, King Lot has shown by his summary that the crimes committed by Maragoz, like the treason of Ganelon, affecting as they do the emperor and the nation in general as well as individuals, constitute what in a later day was to be considered more than simply treason; he therefore suggests in drawing and hanging a punishment which, though a recognized penalty for murder and treason in the thirteenth century, might well have been imposed for what was to be known later as the crime of lese majesty.

In contrast with the protracted deliberation of the judges in *Floriant et Florete* is the precipitate action visited upon Meliatir in *Violette* when, worsted in combat by Girart, he confesses the murder of Ysmaine. Her brother the duke, without even calling for a judgment by the peers to determine the manner of execution, swears that Meliatir shall be drawn and hanged and causes him "to be attached to the tail of a beast of burden, causes him to be drawn vilely to the forked gibbet; then they hang him."[163]

If according to von Amira men were sometimes burned for the crime of murder, we can be sure that for the same offense women were subject to the same penalty. In an episode in *Claris et Laris* a woman escapes punishment although seriously threatened with death in this manner; this is interesting not only for itself but also for its apparent similarity to Celtic custom, which historians agree was obliterated by the spread of Roman institutions in Gaul.[164] In the romance, Sagremors comes across a great press of people about to burn a woman. A bystander tells him what has happened:

> But she was accused of having killed her husband, who had her to wife; of chivalry he had much. The other day the lady arose. Her husband beside her she found dead, who lay beside her in her bed; of this she had little delight in her heart. The news had shortly gone about that the knight was dead; and there was very great grief everywhere throughout the land, for he was of the highest born. When his brother heard the news, you may know that it was by no means pleasing to him. Much he lamented and mourned his brother, and then he sent for the wife. He accused her of having killed her husband. She said that it was nothing of the sort, and that never had she thought of it, and that she would defend herself by the effort of a single knight.[165]

Sagremors, having been refused the request to take the lady home with him since it would be "domage" to burn her, then defeats the brother in combat and frees the lady from blame. Alton points out the similarity between this episode and the one in the *Perceval* in which Gauvain frees a lady threatened with death by fire for having supposedly murdered her brother during the night;[166] but a passage from Caesar's *De bello Gallico* may even further illuminate not only the episode in question but also the reading habits of the anonymous author of *Claris et Laris:*

> when the father of a family, born in a more than commonly distinguished rank, has died, his relations assemble, and, if the circumstances of his death are suspicious, hold an investigation upon the wives in the manner adopted toward slaves; and if proof be obtained, put them to severe torture and kill [burn] them.[167]

That the threatened punishment, if Celtic, is so through literary rather than through legal tradition, may be indicated by the similarity between the two passages in general, and, in particular, by that between Caesar's phrase, "born in a more than commonly distinguished rank," and the poet's "for he was of the highest born."

Unlike the lady in the episode just discussed, in the romance of *Yder* Kay, whose treacherous attempt to poison the hero has been unsuccessful, is not formally threatened with any punishment, though Nuc, Yder's father, has defied him to the death in a judicial duel[168] —a duel which does not take place because, through the mediation of Queen Guenievre, Nuc and Yder are finally reconciled with Kay. Earlier in the same romance, however, after Kay has thrust his lance through Yder's back, Gawain, thinking the hero dead, says, "No law can save him [Kay] from death since one indeed ought to hang a traitor; witnesses there are from many sides."[169] Nevertheless, since Kay has not actually killed his victim and since he has a strong friend in the king, he receives no penalty for a crime which, though definitely treason, is strictly speaking neither homicide nor ambush.

While ambush and particularly truce-breaking were sometimes complained of in the courts,[170] it is more than likely that the knights of romance, in dealing summarily with their waylayers on the spot, closely imitate the doughty flesh-and-blood warriors of twelfth and thirteenth century France. In *Claris et Laris,* when the two heroes have overcome their attackers and when Claris has rescued Lydaine from the old hag who has led them into the ambush, Claris cuts off the hag's hand with his sword.[171] Earlier, after the same two heroes have fought their way out of an ambush prepared for them by the wicked dwarf, they hang him by the neck to a tree.[172] And in *Blancandin* the hero overtakes and cuts the head off the villain who has mortally wounded a knight in ambush.[173]

As a form of treason frequently similar to ambush, brigandage was likewise harshly punished in the Middle Ages, hundreds of brigands and robbers sometimes being executed *en masse* by the Associations of Peace.[174] The chastisement of these pests did not always stop with their extermination, however, and in the romance *Rigomer* we have a good illustration of what further steps were often taken. The viscount and his men, encouraged by Lancelot's killing of a robber-baron in a duel, pursue and slay all the latter's followers. "And the viscount has gone to their house; he causes it to be burnt, and the walls they have pulled to the earth."[175] One may note that for the crime of *escharpelerie* or brigandage the *Établissements de Saint Louis* authorizes the baron to draw and hang the criminal, to burn down his house, to plow under his fields, to root out his vines, and to girdle his trees.[176] Such thorough and complete prosecution of justice as this served not only as a means of publicity but also as a kind of ritualistic moral fumigation.

Crimes not at first clearly recognized as treason, such as *tricherie* in its various forms, were nevertheless as severely punished in the thirteenth century. This may be illustrated by a passage from the *Jostice et de plet:* "The advocates who by their glorious voice cry up cases which are debased, if they do *tricherie* in cases which they have to conduct, they shall suffer the penalty of treason."[177] An examination of other passages in the same book will show that there is little difference between *tricherie* and treason, as Beaumanoir has said, and that there is likewise little difference between their punishments. Consequently we may expect to find such treacherous crimes as forgery and false accusation punished in the romances for the most part as if they were treason.

Although in *Sone de Nansai* the bailiff who has ruined Godefroi de Mesnil through forgery manages to save himself by flight during the trial, he has previously been promised by the queen that he should be "drawn like a false traitor proved,"[178] for he has abused the privileges of his office and has attempted to dispossess another. But even if, according to Beaumanoir, he were to be punished merely as a thief and a cheat, he would die by hanging, unaggravated, however, by drawing.[179] In Beaumanoir's own romance, *La Manekine,* the wicked mother-in-law, who has brought about considerable misfortune to her victims through forgery, does not escape punishment. Instead of putting her to death, however, her son the king, moved by pity, has her walled up in a tower to live the rest of her evil life on bread and water.[180] The imprisonment of high-ranking ladies for less reason than that given in the romance was not unheard of even before Beaumanoir's time, for Luchaire points out that Henry II kept his wife Eleanor a prisoner for many years and that Philip Augustus, abandoning Ingeborg of Denmark the day after their marriage, later shut her up in the tower of Étampes where, having scarcely enough to eat and to wear, she remained for a very long time.[181] But the walling up of the wicked mother-in-law may have been suggested to Beaumanoir by Meleagant's walling up of his elusive prisoner, Lancelot, in Chrétien's *Chevalier de la charette;*[182] if not, then Beaumanoir has perhaps exercised poetic license of a prophetic turn, for in southern Germany and in Switzerland immurement for life in one's own house, though frequently a mitigation of the death penalty and though first recorded in 1337, was not common until the fifteenth century.[183]

Less fortunate than either the bailiff or the mother-in-law is the wicked aunt in the *Comte d'Anjou,* whose fate is decided in the court of the Count of Bourges and his men. The trial reveals less of the subjective side of the medieval philosophy of punishment than that in *Floriant et Florete,* but the punishments suggested, while fewer, are more grisly, and the execution itself is not pretty to contemplate.

> Some judge that the wretched woman should be completely flayed alive, today one member, another tomorrow, until she has neither hand nor foot which is not flayed and salted; and that then the body should be lowered into a foul obscure privy: it is a worthy sepulchre for her. Others say she should be burned, but before all that, she should be larded with pieces of burning fat. The third group say . . . "Let him [the count] cause her to be drawn by horses and all the limbs drawn from her body, and then may he let the dogs eat her." . . .
>
> And says the duke . . . "let the count do with her what he wishes, for one death only will she die."
>
> Says the count, "Cause her to be led under the gibbet, and have brought a great plenty of thorns; and we shall set afire her head of hair and we shall burn her to a cinder."
>
> To the prison they go without waiting. They draw her out by the little ladder; they have put her in a cart;[184] they go straight to the fire, but no creature who may see her mourns for her or has any pity, so ill did she conduct herself toward those who were subject to her. . . . The count caused her to be thrown into the fire; and she was straightly bound. Thus was she forthwith all in flames, for the fire was huge and violent. At the last, with great effort, she uttered an odious and horrible cry. Devils . . . bore her soul to hell.[185]

Although the wicked aunt's initial crime is forgery which because of its purpose is a form of treachery amounting to treason, and although her failure to respond to the king's summons is an offense against royalty, it is doubtful whether the judges who decide her fate have in mind a particular chastisement for a particular crime, for the trial just now recounted differs somewhat from that in *Floriant et Florete:* in the latter a few of the kings make some show of assigning definite reasons for their choice of punishment, whereas in the *Comte d'Anjou* the judges give no reasons whatever for punishments suggested arbitrarily—the arbitrariness, however, is in keeping with a principle which was not altogether foreign to medieval penal laws.[186] Skinning alive by degrees and the salting of the raw flesh advised in the romance, though probably the poet's own elaboration of an ancient aggravation of the death penalty, may have been suggested to him by what occurred about two years before he wrote the romance when Philippe and Gauthier de Launoy, convicted of adultery with two daughters-in-law of King Philip the Fair, were skinned alive, drawn, and subjected to various other tortures.[187] In view of what actually happened to offenders whose crimes involved relatives of the king, and bearing in mind that the romance was written about 1316, is it not possible to see in the judges' proposed flaying of the wicked aunt and in the proposed drawing apart by horses (probably quartering, though the text does not use the word *écarteler*) punishments for another form of lese majesty—namely, disobedience of the king's orders?[188] However, if one wishes to proceed less speculatively to safer ground, one will note, regardless of whatever object the Count of Bourges may have in mind when he decides on his aunt's actual punishment, that forgery was one of the several crimes for which death by fire was inflicted.[189]

If criminals guilty of forgery were subject to punishments like those inflicted upon the wicked mother-in-law and the wicked aunt, naturally those persons convicted of such a form of treason as false accusation or its equivalent were threatened with equally stringent penalties, but not, of course, unless they were convicted, for, since in the twelfth and thirteenth centuries almost every accusation involved the judicial combat, the false accuser had a fair chance not only of getting off scot-free himself but of seeing his victim unjustly punished as well. In the romances, however, the villain is seldom victor, and in *Joufrois* the hero defeats the wicked seneschal who has falsely accused

Queen Halis of adultery with a kitchen boy. Although vanquished, the seneschal refuses to yield himself recreant, and Joufroi cuts off his head.[190] As a matter of fact, Joufroi has taken the only course open to him, for Beaumanoir says that peace cannot be made nor can either party claim quit without the accord of the sovereign; and no sovereign would be likely to grant such accord once a duel had ended in the defeat of one of the combatants.[191] Moreover, it would do the seneschal little good to yield himself recreant, for Beaumanoir further says that in the court of the sovereign the vanquished loses his life, his heritage, and his movable property.[192] We cannot, however, help admiring the seneschal more than the cowardly Nogant in the romance *Durmart,* who, faced with the possibility of having to maintain by force of arms his false accusation of Queen Fenise, saves himself by flight. Since it would be unwise to show himself again in the country, he virtually sentences himself to exile, which in the Middle Ages was indeed one form of punishment for the crime of false accusation.[193] However, in view of the idea of chastising according to the gravity of the offense—an idea possibly behind such laws as required both plaintiff and defendant to remain in prison until one of the two was proved guilty[194]—false accusers may often have been compelled to undergo the punishment intended for the accused, were the latter found innocent. This principle is well illustrated in Chrétien's *Yvain* when the hero clears Lunete of suspected treason against Laudine by overcoming, with the aid of the helpful lion, his three opponents:

> And those men were burned upon the pyre which had been kindled for the damsel's death; for it is right and just that he who has misjudged another, should suffer the same manner of death as that to which he had condemned the other.[195]

Similarly in the *Erle of Toulouse* the two false accusers of Dame Beulybon, of whom the nobles have judged, "The law will that she be brente," undergo the same sort of death after their defeat in combat with the earl, who "anon hym hente, And in the fyre he them brente, Flesche, felle, and boonys."[196] Although in the *Comte de Poitiers* and in *Violette* perhaps neither the Duke of Normandy nor Lisiart intends the lady in question to suffer any particular punishment, they both not only make assertions amounting to false accusations entailing the death penalty but also dispossess their victims by means of false evidence; consequently, after defeat in battle, they both undergo the penalty for treason—drawing and hanging.[197] And in *Guillaume de Dole* the Emperor Conrad would have the calumniating seneschal drawn or burned, but when the interceding nobles beg mercy of the Empress Lienor and suggest that he be sent "across the sea," Lienor, not wishing the seneschal to get off without a "long penance," sentences him to serve the Temple in the holy land.[198]

Another crime, the forcible abduction or violating of a woman against her will, though not treason according to Beaumanoir, was nevertheless punishable, as a case of high justice like treason, by drawing and hanging or, according to other customs, by beheading, drowning, or emasculation.[199] Since rape was, however, a treacherous act which from early times had set in motion the law of vengeance,[200] the romances are not far from right in calling it treason and in threatening its perpetrators with the corresponding punishment. We may say threatening, for in only two of the romances under discussion is the criminal actually punished. Durlus has already been mentioned under the heading of truce-breaking. And in *Blancandin* Blancandin's first adventure is with a knight mortally wounded by the treacherous abductor of his *amie*. Blancandin borrows the knight's armor, overtakes the *amie* and the abductor, who "wished to do his will of her," and after a battle cuts off the villain's head,[201] thus rescuing the as yet untouched lady, who afterward dies of grief upon the corpse of her lover. In *Richars li biaus,* however, the young knight Loys, who has attacked the sleeping Clarisse in her garden, leaps over the wall and runs off when she cries out in the meager hope of learning who the father of her unborn child is. Loys, paying no attention, speeds on his way, for he thinks indeed that he might "lose his life or have his head cut off."[202] Likewise, in the romance *Cléomadés* the deformed African King Crompart, who has been rejected by the youngest sister of Cléomadés and has in revenge carried off on the wooden horse the hero's sweetheart, goes entirely unpunished for his crime, though for an altogether different reason he dies in prison.[203] This crime and the peculiar form of abduction he has hitherto perpetrated in sending Cléomadés off on the wooden horse without having told him how to operate it are apparently treason; this is clear from the conversation between Cléomadés and his father, in which they consider the possibility of Crompart's taking Clarmondine to his kingdom in Africa. Crompart would not be found in his own realm, thinks Cléomadés, because, since his people know of his first offense, they would have the right to stone him, confiscate his possessions, and deprive any heirs of their inheritance should he return before the end of seven years; moreover, even then he could return only if he had made peace with those he had offended and persuaded them to send to his country a letter saying that he had been fully pardoned.[204] It is doubtful whether in the Middle Ages the punishment of stoning was even rarely inflicted for the crime of treason.[205] The exile, however, does seem to be appropriate, for Crompart's crimes are not unlike those of one Eustachius, who in 1270 "propter raptum mulierum, prodicionem, et excessus alios ejectus de villa Cameracensi fuerat et bannitus."[206] But the precise circumstances calling for the chastisements spoken of in the romance suggest that Adenet le Roi has probably made up his law to fit the occasion. The same would appear to be true of the author of *Claris et Laris,* who causes Gawain to tell Mordres, after the latter has unsuccessfully attempted to force a damsel, that anyone who commits such an outrage ought to be "torn apart by four horses."[207] It is noteworthy, however, that afterwards, in the latter part of the fourteenth century, rape came to be regarded as a form of lese majesty,[208] a crime which, as we have already seen, had become punishable by quartering.

Another sex crime, adultery, which in early times was punishable as treason at the discretion of the betrayed husband, while occasionally appearing in the romances under discussion, entails no actual punishment; for the innocent woman falsely accused, like Queen Halis in *Joufrois,* may not only be freed by a champion like Joufroi from the threat of hanging or burning, but may actually live, again like Queen Halis, to indulge, unpunished and unsuspected, in the doubtful practice of courtly love with the man who had earlier saved her life.[209]

Fornication, it has been noted, was definitely punishable by death in early times, though not in the thirteenth century.[210] Consequently it is for this reason that in *Guillaume de Dole* Lienor is at first threatened with death for her supposed liaison with the wicked seneschal. The nephew sent to take her life, however, on arriving at her home, instead of killing her on the spot, brandishes his naked sword and pretends that he will cut off her hair.[211] The shearing off of a woman's tresses was in the thirteenth century a degrading punishment and the mark of a fool.[212] But evidence of fornication must have been difficult to obtain since the practice was very likely to be carried on in secret. Yet the law endeavored to curb free love, reasoning *a posteriori,* for the *Établissements de Saint Louis* stipulates that the gentlewoman who has a child before marriage loses her inheritance.[213] Still, characters like the wicked nurse Gondree in *Violette,* who destroyed two infants she had

had of Dan Baudris, a monk,[214] must have set a questionable example for the *fole fame gentile* who did not wish to lose her inheritance.

Mention of Gondree reminds us of her function as would-be procuress. For her share in betraying Euriaut she is boiled to death in a large cauldron of water over a fire.[215] Her punishment, though an extremely rare one for procuring, is nevertheless symbolic of her betrayal of Euriaut in the bath. In the *Comte de Poitiers* Alotru, who acts as procuress, is punished for spying out small possessions of the countess to give to the Duke of Normandy by having her eyes dug out and her ears and nose cut off and by being put in a nunnery to amend her wicked life.[216] It is of interest to observe that, according to an ordinance of 1228 in Ghent, procuresses were chastised as was Alotru, save that the blinding and imprisonment seem to have been omitted.[217]

The mutilation of Alotru may serve to remind us that, although all criminals in the Middle Ages did not suffer death, some were nevertheless marked for life. For example, while Beaumanoir prescribes hanging for thievery, the *Établissements de Saint Louis* prescribes for a first offense of this sort the loss of an ear, for the second the loss of a foot, and death for the third. Early capitularies stipulated the plucking out of an eye, the cutting off of the nose, and finally death.[218] And as we have already seen, the person convicted of perjury, forgery, or counterfeiting was subject to the loss of his right hand.[219] With the exception of Alotru, scarcely any of the criminals in the romances under discussion suffer punishment of this sort. Yet a few romances reveal fully the social difficulties attendant upon accidental mutilation or self-mutilation.

In *Floriant et Florete* the hero, who has just cut off Maragoz's ear in the judicial combat, taunts him thus: "You are rebuked for stealing, vassal; you have lost your ear."[220] And in *Ille et Galeron,* having received at a tournament an injury which causes the loss of an eye, Ille considers himself disgraced and exclaims, "Alas! What sin has encumbered me?"[221] Had Ille been an Englishman, however, it is probable that he need not have worried, for according to Pollock and Maitland a knight who had lost an ear in battle could obtain an explanatory charter from the king.[222] But perhaps a king like Saint Louis, who frowned on judicial duels and tournaments, would not be likely to grant such a charter. And judging from the manner in which suicide was regarded,[223] one doubts whether anything at all like an explanatory charter would be forthcoming for self-mutilation.

At least Joie, the heroine of Beaumanoir's *La Manekine,* learns to her sorrow the consequences of such a maiming, despite the fact that her father's incestuous desire has to some extent justified her in the act of cutting off her own hand because she knows that a king cannot take for queen a woman "who has not all her members."[224] Instead of burning her as the irate monarch has commanded, however, the kind-hearted seneschal sets her adrift in a boat which is borne finally to Scotland, where in spite of Joie's desire not to reveal her identity and misfortune, the young king falls in love with her. Joie's love for him is overshadowed by the fear that what has saved her from her father may now for the same reason prevent her becoming the Queen of Scotland. Notwithstanding the dictates of his heart, the young king, perhaps mindful of his social position, cannot help entertaining some doubt, however quickly subdued, as to the reason for Joie's mutilation and apparent exile: "Perhaps she has her hand cut off because of her misdeed, and is sent alone upon the sea without company. Because of her misdeed? It cannot be."[225] So for a brief moment the harassing suspicion that perhaps Joie has been thus punished for some terrible crime flits through his mind, but love immediately conquers such a fear. Not so, however, with the king's waspish mother, who, having learned too late of their secret wedding, can think of Joie only as "an abandoned, miserable creature, a fugitive, a woman with one hand."[226] Since she regards Joie only as an unscrupulous and scheming adventuress, we begin to understand not only the reason for her fanatical hatred of the charming stranger, but also in part the reason for her forging of the letters which are to cause Joie even further misfortune. And even the astonished seneschal of Scotland, when he reads the king's supposed command, that Joie and her new-born infant be burned alive, thinks he has hit upon the king's motive when he says, "Perhaps someone has told him, there where he is, where she was born and why she had her hand cut off."[227]

IV

MORAL LAW IN THE OLD FRENCH ROMANCES

ALTHOUGH we have set the law of the romances against the background of actual thirteenth century criminal law and have found them both pretty much in harmony with each other, we are not yet done with crime, for rarely are legal and moral classifications of crime identical, either in thirteenth century France or in the romances. If there was one feature of conduct responsible for the difference between these classifications in the twelfth and thirteenth centuries, it was that of force, concerning which Fundenberg says:

> Force was unlimited and undefined with reference to any high moral standard. Right and wrong were recognized, of course, but they did not determine the application of force, since force was paramount.[1]

It is not difficult to understand that in spite of such restricting and deterrent influences as the law itself, the Church, chivalry, and courtly love—which last had no great salutary effect on morals—the direct application of force as exercised through the law of vengeance or private warfare, and its limited application as exercised in the judicial duel, together with the threat or the fear of force, all must have had bad effects, and must have led eventually, through the conflict of varying social and moral standards, to misconduct of the worst sort. However, if the clashes between vengeance and organized justice, between political and family ties, and between the obligations of love and those of politics did not always result in one sort of crime or another, they led at least to moral confusion—a confusion which romance writers were not slow to make use of.

Although one might at first suppose that when knighthood was in flower a strong sense of personal honor must have helped clarify the confusion just mentioned, one finds on closer examination that instead, honor often served as an incitement to acts of force. Even in Merovingian times insult to the family honor called for violent reprisals through the law of vengeance.[2] And in feudal times, according to Seignobos, honor

> obliged the knight not to endure anything which he thought could possibly be interpreted, by anyone in the world, as a retraction. In practise, it meant the duty of fighting whosoever opposed him in a right to which he pretended.[3]

The prime requisite of honor, therefore, was physical courage best displayed through the exercise of force. In Chapter II we have seen how in actuality Saint Louis, by prohibiting judicial duels within his realm, and how Philip Augustus, by encouraging the legal truce and the *asseurement,* had in a sense tried to limit this notion of honor; and we have also seen that according to Beaumanoir the more refractory were too proud to request the truce or the *asseurement,*[4] probably thinking such a confession of weakness inconsistent with honor. Interestingly enough, the conception of honor described above, together with the attitude of royalty toward it, is clearly set forth in the *Roman de la violette.* When Girart has accused Lisiart of treason and challenged him to the inevitable judicial duel, the Count of Boulogne, representative of the recalcitrant feudal nobility, objects to a peaceful settlement suggested by the Dauphin, the representative of royalty:

> There sat the king under an elm; about him he had many a man. There they began to inform themselves as to whether they might reconcile the two barons without striking a blow. . . .
>
> "This will indeed be no gain for the king, I can assure you, if one makes the other recreant; but if anyone were able to make fair peace and undo this battle, this would be the best conclusion." Thus said the Dauphin.

"By faith," said the Count of Boulogne, "such words are nothing but truce, since there is no right in them. This one accuses him of treason, and everyone has heard the accusation. I was never, by my hat, in any place that I might know of, where for promise or possessions treason might be concealed; rather was it known and open; for scripture testifies, and clerks and monks tell us, that this is the worst sin in which any man can be involved, that of practicing treason. Now hear another matter which theology records: whoever should now make peace and render Girart his land, I tell you for an absolute truth that for this the ill fame of which Euriaut was attainted and into which she had fallen would not be suppressed: and furthermore, the following is well known. He who is accused of treason is then always doubted. Because of this, I cannot know that anyone may have honor if these two make peace, so help me God."[5]

In spite of the Count of Boulogne's questionable knowledge of holy writ and in spite of his doubtful theology,[6] he makes his point perfectly clear; Lisiart can never be shown guilty of treason, Euriaut's reputation can never be redeemed, nor can Girart's honor be vindicated without a conclusive battle to decide the question. Honor—even the lady's honor—calls for force.[7] To quote Briffault, force as a rudiment of conduct was therefore limited by no notion of honor opposed to "treachery, perfidy, deceit, lying, cruelty, and what we should account a degrading lack of self-respect."[8]

Granted that honor had little or no restricting influence over force generally, chivalry and courtly love did not altogether succeed in governing men's conduct and attitude toward women in twelfth and thirteenth century France. In Chapters II and III we have seen that women were frequently subject to forcible abduction or violation and that they were, moreover, not exempt from cruel punishments. Regarding abduction Luchaire says:

Thus the noblewoman was a prize over whom suitors disputed; whom they carried away from father, guardian, even husband! A contemporary of Ida of Boulogne, Stephen, count of Sancerre, carried away an heiress, whom the lord of Trainel had married only a few days before, and made her his first wife. This was the application to marriage of the law that might makes right, which, with all respect to jurists, was the fundamental principle of feudalism.[9]

This philosophy is faithfully reflected in the utterance of Joufroi, hero of the romance *Joufrois,* when he sets eyes on the beautiful Agnes of Tonerre, whose jealous husband keeps her closely confined. Joufroi admits that the husband is right to guard such a treasure. "But," he goes on, "the thief who could steal her should be protected."[10]

As we have seen, the medieval husband was a vengeful person, whether he was actually a cuckold through force or guile or whether he merely suspected himself of being one. The law assisted his revenge by permitting him in rigidly limited conditions to exercise the death penalty upon his unfaithful wife and her lover, but the Church absolutely forbade such legalized murder, though according to Thomas Aquinas it did countenance punishment of the wife in other ways, perhaps such as whipping or beating,[11] and according to Beaumanoir, definitely by the same means for other shortcomings than adultery:

> For it is indeed permitted to the man to beat his wife without death and without injury, when she wrongs him, just as when she is in the way of doing folly with her body, or when she contradicts her husband or curses him, or when she does not wish to obey his reasonable commandments, which an honest woman ought to do. . . .[12]

It is safe to assume that medieval husbands did not hesitate to take full advantage of all their lawful privileges, and that at least in early times some men took even more, if we may credit the story of William of Normandy's kicking a girl nearly to death for the reason that she had refused to marry him because he was a bastard.[13]

In the romances, however, husbands do not often beat their wives.[14] There are, on the other hand, several instances of incivility toward women. Even masculine chastity may rebuff feminine wiles with undue severity, for in the romance of *Yder,* when Yvenant's wife comes up behind Yder and tries to embrace him, he kicks her in the stomach so that she falls in a faint on the floor.[15] For premeditated and unnatural savagery, however, we have only to return to the Durlus episode in *Violette.* After discovering the wounded knight and learning of his abducted bride, Girart sets out in pursuit of the villain and finds him and his men in the act of beating her unmercifully:

The traitor had put her down all naked in her chemise, the felon had despoiled her. Thus three knights held her by the arms very straightly, and very painfully he beat her with a branch of briar so that he left no skin whole upon the flesh.[16]

More to be expected, however, is the action of Harpin in the *Comte de Poitiers.* Having found his outcast aunt in the forest without recognizing her, Harpin strikes her when later, in church, she refuses to marry him: "The châtelain was therefore angry. With his gloves he strikes her upon the nose; her mouth and her chin become red from the spattered blood."[17]

Naturally such treatment as that just described evokes the desire to escape it if possible by any means whatever. And in *Violette* Euriaut, finding herself in a situation similar to that of the Countess of Poitiers, realizes that the simplest way out of her difficulty is, if it works, to tell a lie which paints her in the blackest colors imaginable:

I am a misguided fool, ruined and unfortunate . . . if you knew my affairs you would sooner strike me down, bury me, or burn me in a fire . . . it was three years ago this summer that I became a light woman, and I am called Ligiere, and I am the daughter of a carter. I served yet another trade, for I followed a grave robber, who clothed me in vair, in gray fur, and in silk which he stole; and he loved me, it seemed to me, more than any other creature, until it happened by chance that this robe which I have here he stole the other night at Couci. We were followed for a long time, until by an ambush he was taken and I escaped, who should be condemned. You have no need of such a woman. I wish to recommence my trade.[18]

Thus Euriaut portrays herself not only as the daughter of a carter—suggestion most repugnant—and a woman of easy virtue, but also as the accomplice of a medieval Jerry Cruncher. And her lie succeeds in that she escapes what might have been a forced marriage to the enamored Duke of Metz.

Before we proceed further we shall find it profitable, since we have already observed the twelfth and thirteenth century moral attitude toward force as a feature of conduct, to inquire into the contemporary attitude toward lying, especially since, as we have seen, it may well have been used for the purpose of self-defense. In this connection we may note the significance of Beaumanoir's statement to the effect that in all except criminal cases, where one's life is in peril, both plaintiff and defendant must take an oath of veracity.[19] Further, Thomas Aquinas points out that though all lying is sinful,

if the end intended be not contrary to charity, neither will the lie, considered under this aspect, be a mortal sin, as in the case of a jocose lie, where some little pleasure is intended, or in an officious lie, where the good also of one's neighbor is intended.[20] [Moreover] if the false opinion engendered by the lie be about some matter the knowledge of which is of no consequence, then the lie in question does no harm to one's neighbor: for instance, if a person be deceived as to some contingent particulars that do not concern him. Wherefore a lie of this kind, considered in itself, is not a mortal sin.[21]

Thus it appears that if Euriaut is not altogether morally justified in defending herself from force by a lie which does no harm to another, her moral lapse is at most a minor one.

Just as Euriaut has used falsehood to escape force, so her lover, Girart, uses falsehood colored by force to ward off the unwelcome love of Aiglente, the daughter of the Duke of Cologne. His story follows:

Par Diu, madam, I carried off a woman the other day who was rich with great possessions. She had had a very senseless husband, a knight rich and miserly; a cart could not draw the wealth he had amassed. I thought indeed to have come off very well, since one night I carried off the lady for the wealth which I coveted. I took her to wife. When she was able to escape me she complained to the court; thus she took the land from me. I am not very rich; I dare not go there.[22]

Although Girart's lie harms no one, it is less excusable, on any grounds, than that of Euriaut, yet it helps to show to what extent force as a form of conduct dominated the medieval mind.

As we have just seen, Girart says that he has forced a woman to marry him against her will in order to obtain her property, both movable and real. Should Girart, even though not contemplating matrimony, nevertheless in his lie seize that property by force, the imaginary widow would still have just cause for complaint according to Beaumanoir's technical definition of force as applying either to movable or real property, for, after explaining the term *novel disseizin* as the taking possession of a thing that someone has been peaceably in seizin of for a year and a day, the jurist adds:

If I hold or wish to make use of that of which I shall have been a year and a day in seizin peaceably, and someone takes it away from my possession or from the possession of someone to whom I have entrusted it, or if someone wishes to deprive me of it with a great plenty of people or with arms, so that I do not dare to be there for fear of death, in such case I have good cause to complain of force and *novel disseizin*. You can see that such force constitutes *novel disseizin*, but *novel disseizin* is indeed without force, just as it is said above.[23]

While complaints amounting to what Beaumanoir might call *novel disseizin* and force involving movable property in the romances are rare, the author of *Rigomer* provides us with something like such a complaint, which, though usable for illustrative purposes, is perhaps not technically accurate in all details and is not only settled in a somewhat irregular manner but is at first also complicated by the demands of private vengeance. Mistaking Lancelot for the abductor of a king's daughter, a knight attacks him and in the encounter loses his right hand and his horse. Some days later a relative of the handless knight overtakes Lancelot in the wilderness and accuses him of robbery and felony:

"You will render me this black horse, for you robbed my brother of him and at the same time wounded him—the son of my cousin german, and you cut off his hand. Hence I accuse you of felony."[24]

The accusation puts Lancelot in a bad light, for it omits mention of the fact that he has acted primarily in self-defense. The complaint of robbery, however, seems to take precedence over that of personal injury. And while Lancelot's indignant reply apparently constitutes a blanket denial, it may possibly be calculated to minimize or even nullify the claim of robbery since it stresses treason, which, though perhaps not excluding completely in this instance the idea of robbery, would seem rather to emphasize the fundamental concept of treason—that of secret attack and injury.

"Vassal," says he, "by misprision you have accused me of treason, but ready am I to defend myself if there is one who will take the gages for it, as those shall judge who shall have to judge us."[25]

But even with reference to robbery, however, Lancelot's demand for a legal trial may again reveal him as a shrewd fellow "well acquainted with suits and laws, trials and verdicts." For Beaumanoir says that it is a bad thing if a man having the power does not attempt by force to repossess himself of a horse that has been taken from him by the same means, but that if he cannot regain his horse in this manner he should complain to the court; then, if he can prove that the horse is his, it should be returned to him, but the court should accept no gage from either party, for it is a bad thing if a man has to do battle for his own horse, especially since ravishers and robbers, moreover, would rather take their chances in a combat than be hanged without battle.[26] Consequently, from what Beaumanoir has said, it would appear that since the handless knight himself neither makes any attempt to win back his property by force nor is even present to prove his ownership, his kinsman must therefore offer proof that the horse is not Lancelot's. But since in the wilderness there is no court to which complaint can be made, the two opponents engage to act as mediator in lieu of a regular court a third knight whom they meet and who reveals himself as a practical-minded soul, concerning himself only with the disposition of the horse and forgetting, as has apparently Lancelot's accuser, the matter of vengeance. Turning to Lancelot,

> "Sire," says he, "the judgment I shall tell you quite briefly; there shall be a joust, for I do not wish that it cost more. If he strikes you down from the black horse, he shall have it back quit; and if you strike him down from his, you retain the black horse all quit."[27]

Lancelot wins not only the horse but his opponent's shield as well, thus proving again, in *Rigomer* at least, that might makes right.

In thirteenth century France real property was probably only to a slightly lesser extent subject to seizure by force than was movable property, and complaints involving both must have been common, for Luchaire says:

> There is a proverb: Who has land has trouble. During the reign of Philip Augustus, the abbey of Vauluisant had to undergo no less than forty lawsuits: lawsuits against neighboring religious establishments, against rival churches, and lawsuits against individuals, especially those who had had the sorrow of discovering the bequest of a parent and had refused to give up the heritage.[28]

It is quite possible that some of the forty lawsuits just mentioned, particularly those of the last group, had to do with the forcible seizure of real property[29] and that they were not unlike the following occurrence in *Claris et Laris*. Aglu Desvaus becomes involved in a suit between some nuns and a knight who wishes to deprive them of the abbey which his grandfather had built and endowed for them. The abbess tells her story to Aglu:

"I was the mistress of an abbey which now is cruelly dismayed, for a knight has destroyed it and says that his grandfather gave it of his wealth so largely that even yet he [the knight] is truly the worse for it; so he wishes to take there his eating, his residence, and his drinking; the knight is very rich, but he is very miserly and stingy, taking land from others and behaving ill toward all people."[30]

Although according to the romance the knight has destroyed the abbey,[31] it is obvious that he must have torn it down with a great plenty of people or burnt it down with the aid of a similar following, thus in either case imperiling the lives of any nuns brave enough to remain. They therefore have good cause for complaint of *novel disseizin* by force and actually win their suit through the aid of Aglu, who defeats the offending knight in combat, thus using force to show that its use is wrong.

Although the knight whom Aglu vanquishes is guilty of forcible seizure and destruction of property, his offense is small when compared with the effects of the greatest scourge known to man in all ages—war. And while in the thirteenth century private wars caused considerable damage, political wars, brought about through insubordination, revolt, greed, or lust for power, no doubt caused even more. Force in politics, faithfully described in the *chansons de geste,* is not uncommon in the romances. In the *Comte d'Anjou,* for instance, the young Count of Bourges must leave his wife in order to quell a "high baron of his land who no longer would obey him as he was accustomed to do."[32] And in *Guillaume de Palerne* the powerful Duke of Saxony, after rising against his overlord, the Emperor of Rome, and after laying waste much of the latter's land, is subdued only by a superior military force, captured, and cast into prison, where he dies.[33] In comparison with what Luchaire has to say about war during the reign of Philip Augustus,[34] the author of *Durmart* scarcely exaggerates when he describes the devastation incurred through Nogant's senseless war against his feudal superior, Queen Fenise of Ireland:

Then is he [Durmart] entered into a land where he finds before him the cities burnt and laid waste; fortresses he sees struck down, and churches burnt and fallen in; the mills he finds destroyed and the gardens ravaged. . . . But as he traveled, more than seven hundred men he found on the road, bloody and dead; all naked lay the bodies, and they were not buried; indeed it seemed that there there had been war. The land was so ruined and so evilly laid waste that in twenty leagues without interruption there was not a man or a woman remaining.[35]

Thus, as it has always done, did force in politics take toll of lives and property in thirteenth century life and fiction.

If force was in a sense the basis of honor, if it was responsible for and even formed the content of some kinds of lies, and if it governed to a considerable extent the attitude toward women, property, and politics, its existence in the ordinary relations between man and man may be considered axiomatic, as already pointed out under the heading of vengeance in Chapter II and as may be seen in the recorded accounts of ambushes and truce-breaking.[36] It is in these man-to-man relations, however, that we may begin to see moral confusion and perhaps even crime—characterized for the most part by force—emerge from the conflict between vengeance and organized justice; later we shall see much the same sort of thing resulting from the clashes of other standards or obligations.

To begin with, the issue between vengeance and organized justice was not clear cut, since organized justice was itself to a considerable extent based on vengeance. Moreover, while even from early times the law had generally recognized the difference between an act committed with criminal intent and one that was not so committed, there had at the same time grown up the notion that an injury, even though inflicted through accident or self-defense, called first for vengeance and second for indemnity since such an action, whether voluntary or involuntary, caused the same damage.[37] Brunner has called attention to some of the dilemmas arising from these conflicting principles as related in several older poems and sagas.[38] The situation in the actual law of the later Middle Ages, however, was equally confusing, for on the one hand we find Beaumanoir insisting that a man cannot be put to death for killing another in open warfare or in self-defense,[39] whereas on the other hand, as late as 1374, we find the good magistrates of Abbeville calmly sentencing to be drawn and hanged one Nicaise Thibergue for killing in self-defense and in the presence of witnesses a certain Robert d'Espaigne, who had attacked him with knife in hand about the hour of vespers.[40]

The romances accurately illustrate not only the confusion as to whether an act was voluntary or involuntary but also the confusion as to whether the act should or should not be penalized, and if it should, whether by the authority of vengeance or of organized justice. In the romance *Rigomer* we have seen a few pages back that the accusation against Lancelot reveals at first an attitude of revenge toward a man who has cut off another's hand while defending himself from unwarranted attack. In *Guillaume de Palerne,* however, vengeance is not so easily forgotten in the pursuit of more tangible objects. When in open battle Guillaume kills the nephew of the Duke of Saxony, the Duke, just before capturing Guillaume, cries out:

"Vassal, vassal, indeed you shall pay for the damage that you have done me in my nephew whom you have killed."[41] [To which Guillaume responds:] "You are wrong. I much prefer, faith that I owe you, that I should have killed him than he me, and in self-defense I did it."[42]

Guillaume's plea of self-defense means nothing to the Duke of Saxony, whose attitude differs little from that of the magistrates of Abbeville and whose demand for the reparation of a damage can be met only by the payment of the hero's life. Guillaume's friends see his plight:

They looked towards a hill; they saw him led off straightway; as a thief they [the enemy] were leading him; both his hands they had bound, and banded both his eyes.[43]

But for literary reasons, of course, the friends rescue Guillaume just in the nick of time.

In *Sone de Nansai* the zeal and dispatch with which the high bailiff of Ireland intends to avenge the death of his king, whom Sone has killed in open battle some time previously in Norway, is restrained not by a party of the young warrior's rescuers but by the necessity of permitting him to defend himself in a formal trial at law. In some ways Sone's case is similar to that of Nicaise Thibergue, and it is probable that barring certain limiting conditions he might well have suffered the same kind of death that his counterpart in real life suffered. But let us hear his story from the romance itself. After leaving Norway, Sone is embarrassed to find that Odee, daughter of the King of Norway, has stowed away on board ship in order to be near him. Sone's difficulties increase when, the ship having been blown to Ireland by a storm, he refuses an offer of safety from the ship's captain in exchange for Odee. The treacherous mariner seeks out the bailiff of Ireland, who comes to the establishment of Templars where Sone and his party have taken refuge:

To the master he said: "You shall render up the evil murderer that you have. The king our lord he murdered. For in treason he struck him."

Said the Templar: "This we do not know. A knight we have within. You shall give us everything, and afterward treat him according to law."

. . . Thus he [the bailiff] addressed him [Sone]: "Wretch who murdered my lord and in treason struck him . . . tomorrow you will be drawn like a felon murderer proved."

Said Sone: "You have lied. I never betrayed either him or any other. May God know, if I killed him, in defending my body I did it. With the King of Norway I was, and as a mercenary served him. He came upon him and me; as well as I could I defended us. He came to harass another in order to conquer him, and attacked, causing his own death. And I killed him as a valiant knight, and there was good reason. Nothing but a murderer would be he who for this deed would do me evil. And know well, absolutely, if you should do me any evil for it, that those who are imprisoned [in Norway] you would have brought to their death."

And said the bailiff: "Felon deceiver, proved it is that you are a murderer. Know well that you shall die for it, if by law you do not escape."

The Master Templar replied: "To go to law I brought him here. Now cause the law to judge him as a noble mercenary."

Said the bailiff: "Now guard him; the peers from the castle I have sent for. In the morning we shall bring him before the court. Then afterward we shall draw him." . . .

The peers from the castle came and descended to the temple. . . . The high bailiff spoke very loud; in sight of all he demanded of Sone: "Murderer, have you murdered the good king whose land this is?"[44]

Said Sone: "I did not murder at all; as a valiant knight I took his life in order to save myself and my lord, whom he came to dispossess; and I killed him in his tent in full daylight before many barons. And indeed I offer to prove it with my body. Murder and treason are very strong." Then he went to deliver his gage; according to this he asked to be judged.

The peers looked at one another; the bailiff commanded them that they judge the murderer, by judgment deliver him to him [the bailiff]. The peers said that they would judge him according to law, wrong they would not do in this matter. Said the bailiff, "You shall judge, and I shall hear what you say."

Then they went into a chamber, those who were judges of the fief; together they discussed much and spoke of many judgments.

But there was none so fell that to Sone he might impute treason. Judgment they could not find with which by law they might hurt him. In Norway they had their friends, who had been put in prison in many places. If they gave false judgment, all their friends would have worse.

And said one: "Now let us go and bear him safe judgment."

The peers said: "Declare it very willingly if you wish."

He spoke who for them should speak: "Sire, now listen to us; we have spoken together. This man has killed our lord; and we pronounce our judgment. If he had so much hardihood that he would fight against two, if he could strike them down and vanquish them, all blameless and delivered shall he go away, and also the one whom he brought here. An escort will be given him till he arrive at a good port. He would be drawn and hanged if by these two he were vanquished."[45]

At the advice of the Templar Sone fights—and overcomes—his two opponents. Having proved himself innocent, he then proceeds to thrust an equally distasteful morsel of law down the already gagging throats of the bailiff and the judges when he accuses of treason the mariner who has caused all the trouble, and whom the judges, perhaps in order to save face, convict and sentence to be hanged.

In the preceding episode the death of the King of Ireland would seem to be a public rather than a personal loss such as that of the Duke of Saxony's nephew in *Guillaume de Palerne;* yet the bailiff and the judges exhibit attitudes characterized by all the zeal and vindictiveness of private vengeance. In Abbeville the way of public vengeance was hard upon the man who killed in self-defense. The law in the romance, however, no matter where the author took it from,[46] is rather like the law recorded by Beaumanoir than like that of Abbeville, for in the romance the judges themselves admit that they can find nothing to justify the death penalty for Sone.[47] They are in a peculiar position. Had not the bailiff promised the Master Templar to give Sone a regular legal trial, the judges might have exercised an arbitrary power and caused him to be hanged without trial

—but only after a small war to capture him. They are hampered, however, not so much by the bailiff's promise as by the fear of what might happen to their friends in Norway if they go too far. In their pronouncement, therefore, the judges admit defeat on legal grounds but at the same time proclaim something of the arbitrary power they would like to use in full. When they say, "This man has killed [*tué*, not *mourdri*] our lord," they sidestep the question of murder and treason altogether and merely repeat a fact to which Sone has already twice confessed, having added, however, that his motive was self-defense. Yet the judges reveal their arbitrariness when they proceed to impose the interlocutory judgment demanding that Sone fight against two opponents, not in order to prove his innocence or guilt but in order to satisfy their thwarted desire for revenge, for they apparently do not dream that Sone can win. But even when the combat is over, the queen herself has to persuade the bailiff and the judges that enough is enough. Thus we see in this episode a contest symbolic of the struggle between primitive and modern law, of the confusion between private vengeance and organized justice—a contest in which the hero defends himself from one kind of force by means of another.

The contention between vengeance and organized justice may occasionally have arisen even in games—games of force, to be sure—particularly in the tournament, which Saint Louis and other monarchs regarded with disfavor. Especially was vengeance likely to arise when an accident occurred and a man was killed or wounded in a tournament in which he had taken part of his own free will. Thus in *Rigomer* Gaudiones, after trapping Gawain, threatens him with torture and death for having killed his brother in a tournament:

"Woe the hour in which you saw the death of my brother, for you took his life at the tourney of Roche Florie. Now I shall cause you to suffer much evil, to be torn apart by horses and drawn . . . long you shall lie in prison . . . and when I shall have drawn you, then you shall be burned without any recourse; afterwards the dust will be blown away."[48]

Fortunately for Gawain, the sister of Gaudiones sets him free from prison before he comes to the end intended for him. It is safe to assume, however, that if threats of this kind were not sometimes actually fulfilled, they at least took the form of demands for satisfaction represented to the courts, else Beaumanoir would scarcely have had occasion to write the following:

Sometimes it happens that a game is begun, such as jousting, ball-playing, playing at bars, or other games, and it happens that someone is killed or wounded in the game because a weapon penetrates his heart, or because a lance kills him, or in any other manner. And when such a thing occurs, nothing shall be demanded of him who did it, since in a game which is begun for sport without malevolence, and in which there is an accident through mishap, no recourse shall be had to the court. But it would go otherwise if they became angry in playing, so that the deed was done in a rage, for in such a case he who did it would be judged for the misdeed, for so soon as anger comes, the game ceases.[49]

Gaudiones, of course, has no ground whatever for even a legal complaint since there is no suggestion in the romance that Gawain is guilty of foul play. In *Claris et Laris,* however, the châtelain of Rochele, whose brother has also been killed in a tournament, takes steps which, though not leading to a regular court trial, approximate the procedure implied by Beaumanoir. Instead of attempting to wreak vengeance upon his brother's slayer, he accuses the sponsor of the tournament of treason and tries to establish the motive of malevolence by saying that the tournament had been called only in order that his brother might be put out of the way. The knight Guerrehez defeats the châtelain of Rochele in battle and delivers him to the sponsor, a young girl who, lacking a husband, had without malevolence thought of the tournament merely as an expedient in selecting herself a suitable mate.[50] In this episode, then, and in the two or three immediately preceding we have seen that in the romances the conflict of vengeance versus organized justice is only a reflection of actual conditions; we may conclude that, because of the literary demands of the romances themselves, for those characters caught between the upper and the nether millstones, the results, if inconveniently characterized by force, were perhaps even less so characterized than for people in real life who became involved in similar situations.

We may also conclude that the clash between vengeance and organized justice achieves scarcely less prominence in the romances under discussion than in the *chansons de geste*. We cannot, however, say the same for the clash between political and family ties, for rarely if at all in the romances under discussion does a man have to decide between duty to his king and duty to his family—a dilemma furnishing subject matter for many of the *chansons de geste*. There are in the romances, nevertheless, individuals who do put political ambition above family obligations, as for instance the villain in *Guillaume de Palerne,* who bribes the royal guards to murder his infant nephew in order to become, by an act of force, heir to his brother's throne.[51] Fortunately for the nephew, the plot is discovered in time.

A conflict of obligations quite foreign to the *chansons de geste* proper, yet occasionally appearing in the romances, is the conflict between the obligations of love and those of politics. We are all familiar with the twelfth century stories of Tristram and Lancelot; each hero tries, but with little success, to remain faithful to both king and mistress, and whenever an open breach or an act of force occurs, it is usually brought about through the initiative of the irate king and husband. In one late thirteenth century romance, however, the ideals of courtly love seem to have gone to seed, and instead of serving as a restraining influence, love —certainly not courtly love—serves, as we have already seen, merely as an excuse for acts of force, especially in relations between vassal and overlord. We shall recall that in *Floriant et Florete* Maragoz, rebuked by the queen for his amorous advances, contemplates removing what seems to be the only obstacle in his path. When he hears of the forthcoming hunt, "his heart leaps with joy, for now he thinks to accomplish his desire of his seignior, whom he wishes to murder."[52] How Maragoz succeeds in this wish we already know. Truly, love conquers all, even homage and fealty to one's king! The reader may be inclined, however, to doubt whether love has here completely mastered its victim, for unlike Lancelot, whose mind is for a time unhinged by love, Maragoz surprisingly retains wit enough to seize the kingdom and make a war of revenge upon the lady, who continues to reject him even after the well-meant murder of her husband. The effect of irony is further enhanced when, at Maragoz's trial, King Natalons suggests the lenient penalty of exile instead of the death sentence because the criminal's politically astute though utterly conscienceless act of force was motivated by love, which "causes many a thing to be done that turns to evil and harm; no one can oppose it."[53]

One might go on detailing other conflicts of obligations and other dilemmas in the romances,[54] but enough has been said to show that for the most part a clash of the kinds described above either arises from an act of force or must be settled by one. Little else, we may conclude, could be expected in the fiction of an age when, in spite of church, chivalry, courtly love, and law, force was, no matter what guise it assumed, perhaps the chief feature of honor, of men's conduct toward women and toward each other, and of their conduct in property relations and in politics.

V

LITERARY SIGNIFICANCE OF CRIME AND CRIMINALS IN THE ROMANCES

SINCE many criminals of the romances exercise force in order to accomplish their evil purposes, we may reasonably assume that similarity of act argues a monotonous sameness in mind and personality. A moment's reflection will reveal some of the criminals who resort to force as entirely lacking in moral scruples of any kind but possessing a certain ingenious animal cunning that can hardly be called subtlety of character; others, having little individuality, may appear simply as uninteresting but obnoxious minor figures. In *Floriant et Florete,* Maragoz, of whom we have just spoken in the preceding chapter, is in some ways naïve, but is also crafty and brutal; in *Violette* Durlus, who wounds a knight and beats his bride, is an unimportant person whose only distinction lies in cruelty rather than in shrewd villainy. Readers familiar with the romances will be likely to recognize in both of these criminals much that is conventional and will ask whether any of the villains in the romances conduct themselves as self-sufficient individuals independent of plot, and whether any of them is individual enough to escape recognition as a disguised stock type borrowed from other romances or from some other literary form, such as the *chansons de geste.*

One sure indication of individuality or its absence in the character of a villain lies in the analysis of his motive for crime. Lust, avarice, and the desire for revenge, often utilizing brute force merely as a tool, are perhaps the commonest of motives; in themselves they reveal little, yet frequently they are guided by personal idiosyncrasies which reveal much of character. For example, it is not always the spirit of reprisal that alone constitutes the motive for revenge; that motive may be compounded partly of other elements —jealousy, cowardice, a hopeless sense of inferiority, or even unbalanced mother love.

In the romance of *Guillaume de Dole* jealousy is the prime weakness in the character of the wicked seneschal, who, apprehensive of losing his position at court and unable gracefully to brook a rival near Emperor Conrad's throne, tries to discredit Guillaume by insinuating that his sister is not a virgin. Moreover, the seneschal's method of achieving his maliciously conceived vengeance is evidence of a further flaw in his character—cowardice, for only a coward would knock a woman down in the attempt to strike a man over her shoulder. Although the seneschal's manner of vengeance is inexcusable, we can all sympathize to some extent with his desire to retain his position of favor, for no one wishes to lose what he has. Certainly the Duke of Normandy in the *Comte de Poitiers* and Lisiart in *Violette* do not wish to lose their lands because in a moment of thoughtlessness they have accepted wagers to seduce ladies whose virtue is incorruptible; and though the seneschal's strategy appears to be the strategy of a cornered rat, as theirs really is, his action is less justified than theirs since their need for self-preservation is greater and more immediate than his. The offenses perpetrated by Lisiart and the Duke of Normandy, conventional as they are in the romances, are worth little as indices of personality, for they represent, so to speak, something like reflex action. The seneschal's misdeed, on the other hand, is the result not only of the requirements of plot, but essentially of an inherent weakness in character which, while it might have become scarcely less disastrous in its development than Iago's plotting against Cassio, nevertheless stamps him as an individual.

Although in the seneschal's personality cowardice plays second fiddle to jealousy, in the character of King Nogant of the romance *Durmart* it leads the whole orchestra. This fact alone heightens the individuality of Nogant, for with the exception of Kay, who is also occasionally something of a fool, there are very few physical cowards in the romances; those who perpetrate cowardly acts are, like Maragoz in *Floriant et Florete,* for example, seldom afraid to fight when they have to, even though they may expect almost certain defeat. Nogant is not one of these, however, for though he takes a sparrowhawk to present to his cousin, Queen Fenise, he is not only afraid to fight for it, but shortly afterward is dastard enough to attack the wounded Durmart, who has fought for the sparrowhawk and killed his opponent in doing so. When Durmart, wounded as he is, shows signs of fight, Nogant becomes so frightened that he is easily unhorsed. It is for these exhibitions that Fenise twits him with cowardice. We have already seen in Chapter III how in revenge he first lays waste her land and then accuses her of heresy. When his falsehood is unmasked and a duel with Durmart is proposed, King Nogant, trembling with "paor fine," says that it would be a pity if he fought Durmart because he would surely kill him; but since Durmart is only a king's son and not a king, Nogant disdains to enter combat with him. Josefent, Durmart's father and a king in his own right, takes the wind out of Nogant's sails by offering to crown Durmart at once. Under pretext of seeking advice of his counsellors, however, Nogant, already laughed at, slips out quietly and gallops off for dear life. In him we have perhaps the most consistent craven in the literature of the romances. Huge, almost Falstaffian in physical proportions and in boastfulness, yet lacking both discretion and valor, Nogant is at heart a humorless villain. A curious combination of nefarious treachery and unconscious buffoonery, with abject cowardice the dominant weakness in his character, Nogant is almost unique among the bad men of the romances.

A unique bad man, the ugly, hunch-backed King Crompart of Africa, appears in the romance *Cléomadés*. The uniqueness of his villainy arises from what today we should call an inferiority complex. Sensitive of his deformity, he realizes that he cannot succeed in the role of lover. Therefore, when he and two other African kings fall in love with the three fair daughters of King Marcadigas of Spain, Crompart, who has the "cuer soutill," suggests, in order to improve his own chances, that each of the three colleagues prepare a rich gift to King Marcadigas before broaching the subject of marriage with his three daughters. Bearing in mind the inevitable prejudice that he must overcome, Crompart further suggests that the gifts be presented to Marcadigas on his birthday, when he is likely to be in a generous mood and less apt to quibble. On the day in question the three kings present their gifts to Marcadigas, who in return offers them what they will in the way of lands, castles, or towns. It is then that Crompart, acting as spokesman for all three, asks for the hands of the princesses in marriage. Naturally Marcadigas temporizes because of Crompart's disgusting appearance, but, not knowing how to extricate himself from the difficulty, agrees to let each king take his choice of the daughters after he has demonstrated his gift. When the first two kings have successfully performed their demonstrations and chosen the two older daughters, Marine, the youngest, faints. Reassuring her, her brother Cléomadés, angry with Marcadigas for betrothing her to such a creature as Crompart, insists on a demonstration of the latter's gift, a flying horse of ebony. Crompart, afraid of Cléomadés and thinking to get him out of the way, turns a peg on the ebony horse, causing it to fly off with Cléomadés on its back. Marcadigas immediately claps the villain into prison. Having meanwhile learned by experiment how to operate the horse, Cléomadés returns home after a few days' absence and frees Crompart, who does not, however, go back to Africa because of a law which exiles criminals like him for seven years. But his villainy is not yet ended. When from a second trip to Italy Cléomadés comes back with the beautiful Clarmondine, whom he has met and fallen in love with during his first unexpected flight on the ebony horse, he alights with her in a garden near the palace. Leaving her there to rest, the hero then goes in search of his parents, sisters, and friends in order to prepare a royal reception for his sweetheart. At this point Crompart, who now makes his living by gathering medicinal herbs in the garden, frightens the girl, who calls out for her lover. Joyful at the double opportunity for revenge against Cléomadés and for obtaining a better than fair substitute for Marine, Crompart, under pretense of being a messenger from Cléomadés and in spite of his hideous appearance, induces Clarmondine to mount the flying horse with him. This is his last act of villainy, for though he succeeds in separating the lovers, later, after he has alighted with Clarmondine near Salerno, Crompart, refusing to answer King Meniadus's questions, is put in prison, where he dies. Here indeed is a villain whose character does not conform to a common pattern. His physical handicap has produced in him a sense of inferiority for which he tries to compensate by the machinations of his "subtle heart." His suggestion of the gifts for Marcadigas, his selection of the latter's birthday for the date of presentation, his acting as spokesman—all confirm the impression that the chief weakness of his character lies in his sensitiveness to his own deformity. And finally, the abduction of Clarmondine shows him to be as much an individual in his depravity as that other hunch-backed monarch of literary renown, Richard III, who said, "Since I cannot prove a lover, . . . I am determined to prove a villain."

In Beaumanoir's *La Manekine* the wicked mother-in-law is a character far from unique, yet her treachery is the result of a curious mixture of plain common sense and emotional instability—a mixture which proves her to be no less an individual in her way than Crompart is in his. Probably no mother of an only son can entirely escape some emotional upheaval when she sees the young man's affection turn toward another woman. And when the other woman appears to be of doubtful reputation, the mother's possessive and protective instincts are bound to react more strongly. The fact that Joie is a handless and apparently exiled waif has, as we have already seen, given pause to the young King of Scotland himself. But his mother, perceiving the growing fondness between the two, even threatens Joie with death if she continues seeing the king. Her common sense tells her that since people do not get exiled or have their hands cut off for nothing, an obvious criminal like Joie, who refuses to tell anything about herself, is certainly no match for her son. The queen mother's threat, therefore, may be merely a gesture—and according to her lights a sensible one —to frighten off a designing adventuress. Were the queen mother a little less sensible and a little more shrewd, she would foresee the result of such a threat. But having thus forced the lovers into each other's arms, she is completely outraged at their secret marriage in defiance of her will. Her common sense now gradually gives way before the secret, relentlessly corrosive force of a powerful and acid emotion—a consuming hatred of the usurper that can be satisfied only by the fulfillment of the threat which may at first have had no serious meaning. Hence later, when the grandchild is born, she forges a letter which, except for the failure of the seneschal of Scotland to obey its commands, would have led to the death of both Joie and her infant son. The queen mother's motive, as we have seen, is at first well founded. In fact, it is much better founded than that of her counterpart, the wicked aunt in the *Comte d'Anjou,* who has no evidence whatever that her nephew's young wife is a criminal, for the latter, instead of cutting off her hand as Joie has done in *La Manekine,* has run away to escape, like Joie, an incestuous marriage with her father; yet the aunt forges a letter demanding the death of the girl and her baby merely because she suspects the heroine to be of low origin and because she is afraid that her new grandnephew, who would eventually inherit her lands, is therefore "vilain." In *La Manekine,* the mother-in-law's treachery, however, achieving the unhappiness of the King of Scotland and all but the death of his wife and child, is the direct outcome of the utter and complete frustration of the maternal instinct, the extravagance of which is the one weak spot in the queen mother's bright armor of common sense, propriety, and convention.

In one way the term *conventional* suggests that the wicked mother-in-law belongs to a type—a fact verified by the host of wicked mothers-in-law appearing throughout the various kinds of medieval narrative literature.[1] The same is true of the wicked seneschal[2] and other typical villains in the romances. But, as shown in the preceding pages, at least some of these figures are individuals as well as representatives of types, as were the Canterbury pilgrims. Although it is risky to generalize, we may say that the villains of the romances differ considerably from those of another literary genre from which a great deal of the material of the romances comes—the *chansons de geste.* Gautier has pointed out that the villains of the *chansons de geste,* like the tyrants of melodrama, are objects of universal hatred painted in black, and in deep black too.[3] Comfort, moreover, tells us that there is an element of fate in the sad lot of these traitors and that some of the later writers of the *chansons de geste* content themselves with the remark that their traitors cannot help themselves because they are of the race of Ganelon.[4] If we may invoke a paradox and speak of villains in terms of heroes, then the villains of the epic *chansons de geste* are a little like such epic heroes as Odysseus, whose course in life is guided (in a direction different from that taken by the traitors of the *chansons de geste,* of course) by forces outside of him, by Poseidon, by Athene—in short, by destiny. On the other hand, again bearing in mind the hazards of generalizing, we may say that at least a few of the villains of the romances resemble somewhat the Aristotelian hero of tragedy, whose downfall is due to an error in judgment; and Aristotle would probably have been the first to grant that errors in judgment are brought about through lack of proper balance among the internal forces of character. It would appear, then, that although most of the poets of the *chansons de geste* are willing to attribute all evil to membership in the tribe of Ganelon, some of the romance writers, on the other hand, are not satisfied with portraying mere puppets of destiny but, on the contrary, are more keenly analytical of character and dig a little deeper for such motives for action[5] as we have seen in the character of the wicked seneschal in *Guillaume de Dole,* of the coward Nogant in *Durmart,* of the deformed Crompart in *Cléomadés,* and of the wicked mother-in-law in *La Manekine.*

Not all writers of romances, however, are bent on making their characters consistent either as heroes or villains, and for various reasons. It may seem a little short of miraculous to find a dyed-in-the-wool horse thief like Fel de la Garde of the romance *Durmart* suddenly leaving his old error and treading in the path of virtue with nothing but his conscience and maybe the fear of Durmart as his guide. Yet such things do happen, and the example is salutary. To the modern reader the apparent inconsistency in the character of Emperor Conrad in *Guillaume de Dole,* who connives with ardent wooers at outwitting jealous husbands but who flatly rejects the idea of marriage with a girl reported to be unchaste, may be explained not by Conrad's accession to a higher morality but by what is known as the conventional double standard.

Sometimes, though, not even the double standard can entirely explain away anomalies in character. In the romance *Joufrois,* for example, the hero's actions, both moral and immoral, are the direct result of the author's mixture of plots—conventional plots of widely differing types. In the first episode Joufroi defeats and kills the wicked seneschal, who has falsely accused Queen Halis of adultery with a kitchen boy. In another episode Joufroi, masquerading as a religious hermit, hoodwinks the husband of the beautiful Agnes of Tonerre and has an amour with the lady herself. In the last episode the hero, with his friend Robert, returns to the court of Queen Halis, whose honor he has previously defended but who now makes an assignation with him for a certain hour during the night. When she is a little delayed, the impatient Joufroi gets up to listen at the door for her footsteps. Robert, having meanwhile slipped into Joufroi's bed, tells him on his return that he is probably confused from too much drink. Thinking therefore that he has lost his way in the dark, Joufroi proceeds to Robert's bed. Consequently, when Queen Halis arrives, it is Robert who welcomes her. Some time later Robert not only amazes her by graciously informing her of her mistake, but even goes to tell Joufroi that the queen awaits him in his bed. When the two embrace hastily, and when Joufroi tells Queen Halis how Robert has tricked them both, she laughs, and the lovers take their full joy. Although the situation in the first episode of the romance *Joufrois* occurs often in medieval narrative literature, it is probably only a slight variation of an old *chanson de geste* theme, such as appears in *Macaire.*[6] The second episode mentioned stresses courtly love and its devices, as in romances like *Flamenca* and the

Châtelain de Coucy. And the humorous off-color situation in the last episode smacks unquestionably of the *fabliaux,* perhaps being a clever variant, on a higher social plane, of similar incidents in *Le Clerc et son frere laboures*[7] or *Trubert.*[8] No matter how much we may relish the profound irony of the conclusion, we must admit that the author of *Joufrois,* in achieving his literary purpose, has had to make his hero a criminal, who if caught in the act would be subject to immediate death according to the legal standards of his day. While Joufroi is none the less a criminal, the poet has saved his life by transferring him bodily from the plot of a *chanson de geste* to that of a *fabliau* representing a literary type in which virtue is seldom rewarded and vice rarely punished. Joufroi is, nevertheless, a conventional though composite figure, and what is true of him may also, for similar reasons, be true in other ways of other criminals, whether heroes or villains, in other romances.

By this time it must have become perfectly obvious to the reader what part criminals and crime play in the structure of the twenty-odd romances thus far discussed. Almost two-thirds of them belong to a group called the society romances, most of whose plots, according to Miss Barrow, fall into a more or less definite pattern.[9] This plot formula, corresponding to the five stages of courtly love, has five divisions, the first three of which bring two young people together and result in their falling in love; the fourth stage is a period of complication and trial in which the lovers become separated or estranged; and in the fifth stage the last obstacle between them is generally removed in decisive fashion. Although some exceptions like *Joufrois*[10] are inevitable, a plot scheme having so fundamental a basis as a complication and its resolution is bound to apply to other narrative types besides the society romances. In fact, it might roughly apply to most of the romances we have been discussing, for though we cannot conveniently label them romances of crime, we may say that crime in one form or another is often the complicating agency that brings about the temporary separation of the lovers. If it is not adventurous deeds of prowess calling often for the righting of a wrong or for the punishment of some incorrigible villain—if it is not such deeds that separate the hero from the heroine until he considers himself worthy of her or until she herself is in dire distress, then it is often more directly, as in *La Manekine,* a crime of major proportions that casts its ominous shadow between the lovers. And sometimes, as in *Guillaume de Dole,* the chief interest of a romance may be shifted from the love element itself to the solution of the difficulties arising between the lovers—in other words, to crime and its punishment.

VI

SUMMARY

IN CONCLUDING this study of crime and punishment in the romances, we shall observe that while there is no particular group which may be called romances of crime, crime nevertheless has an important function in the narrative development of many romances. The criminal himself, moreover, though he may represent a conventionalized type drawn from the *chansons de geste* or even the *fabliaux,* often acts as an individual on motives psychologically sound. We must also remember that his personal psychology is for the most part in keeping with the moral psychology of his age, which, as shown in Chapter IV, is dominated by force. It may be well, however, to remind ourselves that in twelfth and thirteenth century France not all acts of force were considered criminal. Private warfare, we know, was entirely legal; and even though Beaumanoir treats the seizure of property by force as quasi-criminal, the *Très ancien coutumier de Normandie* regards it more as a case for adjudication by civil authorities.

Although the subject of civil law in the romances appears to be one worth investigating, we have concerned ourselves chiefly with criminal law, and we have seen in Chapters II and III that the punishment inflicted upon the convicted criminal of the romances is, like that inflicted upon his counterpart in real life, often harsh and brutal. Moreover, except for occasional distortion for literary effect, the frequently illogical but generally formal procedure through which the criminal is convicted reflects with a fair degree of accuracy the actual procedure used in the twelfth and thirteenth centuries. In these two chapters we get, on the whole, an understandable picture of the forms and spirit of medieval criminal justice and also some idea of what constituted certain crimes, such as treason. The reader may have felt at times that some of the offenses called treason in the romances could hardly have been so regarded in actual law. Beaumanoir's definition of treason, however, is capable of broad interpretation, especially since it emphasizes the intent rather than the act itself. It is difficult to say whether or not the emphasis on intent was due in part to the influence of canon or Roman law. And while the romances appear to stress the intent of the traitor as much as Beaumanoir does, they may do so as much for literary reasons as for legal ones.

If we perhaps cannot deny the complete absence of the influence of canon and Roman law in the romances as Gautier has denied that of Roman law in the *chansons de geste,* we may say that the criminal law of the romances is scarcely less Germanic in background than the custumals upon which it seems to be based. This appears particularly true if we remember that, though scholars, men of religion, and men of law were among those who wrote the romances, they wrote chiefly for an aristocratic class of people whose interests lay in the tense and concrete drama of love, war, and criminal intrigue—not in the subtle abstractions of legal or moral systems which in effect were somewhat foreign to their native cultural heritage.

Although the present study has not attempted to exhaust the subject of crime and punishment, it is hoped that the detailed presentation of the facts, together with some account of their relationship to one another, will help sketch in more clearly a small part of the extensive and sometimes obscure background of the Old French romances. It is hoped also that someone may be encouraged to examine the French romances further or to make a similar investigation of the Middle English romances.

APPENDIX

APPENDIX

Claris et Laris

BECAUSE he has fallen in love with Lydaine, the young wife of the century-old King Ladont of Gascony, and since he does not wish to be disloyal to the king, Claris sets out with Lydaine's brother Laris to win fame as a knight.

The two young warriors encounter a dwarf, who leads them to a castle where seven robbers attack them. After they kill all but two, Claris and Laris rescue Yvain from prison. Meanwhile the dwarf brings from the forest twenty-five more thieves, fourteen of whom the three knights kill, the rest seeking safety in flight. Claris and Laris then seize the dwarf and for his treachery hang him from the limb of a tree.

After other adventures the two heroes are recalled to Gascony, which has been laid waste by the King of Spain. Claris and Laris assist in putting the Spaniards to rout, and Claris wins Lydaine's promise to marry him upon the death of her aged husband. With several of Arthur's knights who have helped them in the war, Claris and Laris set out for Britain, where they are to wait until Lydaine is free. On the way, Laris becomes mysteriously separated from them. Claris and his companions decide to find Laris before going on to Arthur's court.

In the search they in turn separate, and one of them, Gaheriez, spends the night with a hermit. Several thieves come to rob the hermit's chapel, but Gaheriez kills them one by one as they come out the door and hangs their bodies upon two trees.

Another of Claris's party, Sagremors, sees a crowd of

people about to burn a woman. He learns that the lady's husband has died in bed at night, and that the dead man's brother has accused her of murder. Although she has protested her innocence and has asked for a champion to defend her, no one offers to fight for her. Sagremors defeats the brother and frees the lady from blame.

Eventually reunited, Claris and Laris later participate in a tournament held by King Arthur, but Laris, wounded, is brought to Guinivere's chamber to be cared for by the ladies. Here he falls in love with Marine, Yvain's sister. His happiness is cut short, however, by the news that Ladont's death has emboldened the Spaniards to make a second invasion into Gascony and to carry off the widowed Lydaine to Spain. Claris and Laris, with Arthur's army, defeat the Spaniards a second time and rescue Lydaine, whom Claris now marries amid great rejoicing.

Laris, however, longs for Marine, and the sympathetic Claris decides that they shall return to Britain to win the lady for Laris. Lydaine insists on accompanying them. The three arrive at a castle the lord of which has the custom of lying with a different woman each night. Upon the wicked host's attempt to enter Lydaine's chamber, he is attacked by the two heroes and killed in the ensuing melee. The next day, after fighting their way through the dead host's retainers, Claris and Laris, with Lydaine, are led into an ambush by the host's hag-like mother, whose right hand Claris cuts off as punishment after the ambuscaders have been put to flight.

At length the two companions and Lydaine arrive at Arthur's court, only to learn that Tallas, a disappointed suitor of Marine's, besieging her in her father's city, threatens to take her by force. Claris, Laris, Yvain, and others go to the rescue. During a skirmish Laris is captured and carried off to Denmark by Tallas. Claris, with twenty-nine knights, sets out in search of Laris. The party breaks up into three groups of ten each. Claris, with the first group, comes to ten roads in the forest. The ten knights separate, each going a different way.

The seventh knight of the first group, Guerrehez, comes to a castle the lady of which, wishing to have a husband, has offered to accept the winner of a tournament, in which, accidentally, a man is killed. His brother accuses the lady of treason, saying she has called the tournament in order to have her victim slain. Guerrehez defeats the brother in a duel and delivers him to the lady.

The fourth knight of the second group, Gales, finds a damsel weeping over the severed head of her lover. She seeks vengeance for his death. Gales appeases her by cutting off the murderer's head, which the damsel attaches to the tail of her horse and drags to her castle, where she has it hung from a gibbet.

Mordres, the fifth knight of the second group, having attempted to force a damsel, is about to be hanged by her two wrathful brothers. Gawain rescues Mordres, but admonishes him that the forcing of a woman is cruel treason, for which a man ought to be torn apart by four horses.

The seventh knight of the third group, Aglu Desvaus, encounters some nuns whose abbey has been destroyed by a knight. The man claims the property on the ground that his grandfather, having founded and endowed the abbey, has thus impoverished the heirs. Aglu defeats the knight in a judicial duel and establishes the legality of the nuns' ownership.

After numerous adventures Claris and the twenty-nine knights are ultimately reunited, and in the disguise of hermits, they enter Tallas's castle, rout the defenders, and free Laris. A general war follows, in which Arthur defeats Tallas. Thus, when still other obstacles are overcome, the way is finally cleared for the long-delayed marriage of Laris and his sweetheart, Marine.

Cléomadés

A hunch-backed monarch from Africa, King Crompart, and two other African kings, having presented rich gifts to the King of Spain, in return demand his three daughters in marriage because he has promised them anything they wish. Marine, the youngest, faints when she learns that Crompart is to be her husband. Her brother Cléomadés mounts the flying horse of ebony—Crompart's gift—to see if it is all that it should be. The golden trumpeter—gift of one of the other kings—blows his horn to announce treason, but no one pays any attention, and Crompart causes the horse to fly off with Cléomadés. The villain is put into prison at once. Meanwhile, having learned how to operate the horse, Cléomadés alights in Italy, where he falls in love with the king's daughter, Clarmondine. Unfortunately, he is seized and condemned to be hanged for his intrusion. Receiving permission to die on his horse—a concession to his nobility—Cléomadés mounts and flies back to Spain, where he liberates the now disgraced Crompart, who does not even dare to return to his own country. After a short time Cléomadés returns to Italy and has little trouble in urging Clarmondine to elope with him. Alighting in a garden near the palace in Spain, Cléomadés leaves his sweetheart in order to announce their arrival to his family. But Crompart, who now gathers herbs in the garden, persuades Clarmondine that he is a messenger from her lover and induces her to mount the flying horse with him. The golden trumpeter again announces treason, and again no one heeds his warning. They alight near Salerno, where King Meniadus imprisons Crompart for refusing to answer his questions. After a long search Cléomadés finds his sweetheart and at last they, together with five other couples, are happily married.

Comte de Poitiers

The Count of Poitiers, confident of his wife's virtue, wagers his land that the Duke of Normandy cannot seduce her. The duke tries, but fails. Through the agency of a wicked nurse, however, he secures some of the countess's intimate possessions, which he pretends are evidence of his conquest. Disgraced at the loss of his land and the apparent infidelity of his wife, the count leads her into the forest to kill her, but instead abandons her to her fate. She is found by her nephew, who, not recognizing her, attempts to marry her by force. Meanwhile the Count of Poitiers, having learned of the duke's treachery, sets out in search of his wife. The two are reunited, and the Duke of Normandy, accused of treason and proved guilty in a judicial duel, is hanged and drawn, and the wicked nurse is mutilated and imprisoned in a convent.

Erle of Toulouse

Two nobles, rebuffed in their advances to the queen, persuade young Sir Antore to conceal himself in her chamber. The two villains then enter, kill Antore, and accuse the queen of adultery. The court, in judging her, can find no law to save her from death until an old knight points out that no one has ever before found any fault in the queen and that Antore was killed before he could say a word in self-defense. In the following judicial duel the Erle of Toulouse defeats the queen's two accusers and burns them in the fire intended for the queen herself.

Joufrois

In a judicial duel Joufroi defeats and beheads the seneschal of England, who has falsely accused Queen Halis of adultery with a kitchen boy. Upon returning home to Poitiers, Joufroi, in the guise of a religious hermit, hoodwinks the jealous husband of Agnes of Tonerre and has a successful amour with the lady herself. In England again, this time with his companion Robert, Joufroi lives lavishly, and to offset his rash spending, he marries the daughter of a wealthy bourgeois for her dowry. Upon learning that Poitiers has been attacked by a hostile lord, Joufroi prepares to leave England. He persuades King Henry to espouse his bourgeois wife to an impoverished nobleman. Then, for three days before his departure, Joufroi carries on a secret love affair with Henry's wife, Queen Halis—an affair which is marred only at the beginning by the amusing deception contrived by Joufroi's companion, Robert. Upon Joufroi's return to Poitiers, he defeats the invading nobleman and marries the latter's daughter.

La Manekine

Because she knows that a king may not marry a woman without all her members, Joie cuts off her hand in order to forestall an incestuous marriage with her father. Irate, the latter orders her to be burnt, but the sympathetic seneschal sets her adrift at sea instead. On Joie's arrival in Scotland the young king falls in love with her and, in spite of his mother's prohibition, marries the young lady. When his son is born, the King of Scotland, away from home, can hardly believe the letter (forged by his mother) saying that Joie has given birth to a devil's offspring. The king writes ordering his seneschal to take no action till his return. But the queen mother forges a letter to replace this one also. The dumbfounded seneschal of Scotland does not burn Joie and her son, as the forged letter commands, but sets them adrift in a boat. Upon the king's return the mystery is cleared up, and the wicked mother is immured in a tower for life. After a long search the king eventually finds his wife and child in Rome.

Rigomer

Lancelot determines to follow a damsel who, having come to Arthur's court, has left abruptly because no one has asked the name of her lady or the land from which she has come. After thirty days Lancelot finally arrives in Ireland, where he has many adventures.

Making his way to a city in which everyone is lamenting, Lancelot learns from the viscount that a robber baron has set this day to carry off the viscount's daughter if no one will defend her against him. Lancelot accepts the challenge and cuts off the villain's head upon his refusal to yield himself recreant. The viscount and his men pursue and kill the remaining robbers and also burn down and destroy their stronghold.

Learning from the viscount that the land he seeks is called Rigomer, Lancelot presses forward on his journey, stopping the next night with a lord who tries to discourage him from his quest and who suggests that instead Lancelot remain to defend a widow whose former husband's nephew wishes to deprive her of her dowry. Since the widow has said things in court which she could not retract, Lancelot cannot act as her legal adviser, but he does help her by defeating the nephew in a judicial duel.

Continuing on his way, Lancelot rescues the daughter of the King of Cork from a man about to rape her. As Lancelot is conducting the lady to her father, one of the king's men, in search of her, mistakes Lancelot for the abductor and attacks him. In the encounter Lancelot cuts off the man's hand and takes away his horse. After restoring the lady to her father, Lancelot goes on toward Rigomer. A relative of the handless knight overtakes Lancelot and accuses him of robbery and felony. Lancelot denies the charge. A third knight, to whom they take their dispute, suggests a joust as judgment. Lancelot wins, thus retaining the horse as his property.

Finally Lancelot reaches Rigomer, where by enchantment he is made prisoner. Meanwhile the knights whom he has conquered arrive at Arthur's court and tell their stories. Gawain and others set out to free Lancelot.

In Ireland Gawain meets the knight Gaudiones, who turns tail upon learning Gawain's name. In full pursuit, Gawain follows to Gaudiones's castle, where he is taken prisoner and threatened with drawing, hanging, and burning for having accidentally killed Gaudiones's brother at the tourney of Roche Florie.

The sister of Gaudiones liberates Gawain, who eventually arrives at Rigomer, where he frees Lancelot and wins the high regard of Dionyse, the lady of Rigomer. After Lancelot, Gawain, and the rest of Arthur's men return home, there are still other adventures, and the romance comes to an indeterminate conclusion.

Sone de Nansai

Sone, unsuccessful in a love affair which he tries to forget, goes abroad in search of adventure. In Norway he assists the king against an invading army of Scotch and Irish and in open battle kills the King of Ireland.

When the war is over, Sone, now wishing to return to the lady he loves, embarks for home. But Odee, daughter of the King of Norway, has stowed away on board ship in order to be near him. In a storm the vessel is blown out of its course. It stops at Ireland, where the treacherous sea captain offers Sone safe conduct in exchange for Odee. Sone refuses and, with Odee, takes refuge in an establishment of Templars. The captain, however, informs the bailiff of Ireland, who accuses Sone of having treasonably murdered the King of Ireland. A legal trial follows, and Sone proves his innocence by defeating two champions in a judicial combat.

After harrowing adventures at sea, Sone returns Odee to

her father, but again takes leave of Norway. Nevertheless, touched by Odee's devotion, he promises to return. At home Sone finds that though the lady of his choice now reciprocates his love, marriage with her is forbidden because she is his mother's god-daughter. By means of a pilgrim he sends a message to Odee.

Godefroi de Mesnil, husband of Sone's cousin, having signed a note for 2,000 *livres,* is impoverished by the royal bailiff, who has forged the note to read 100,000 *livres.* Sone informs the king that Godefroi has been falsely dispossessed, and a day is set for a judicial investigation, but the treacherous and thieving bailiff absconds.

Later Sone goes again to Norway, where, upon marrying Odee, he is crowned king. Some years afterward, named emperor by the Pope, Sone makes war against the Saracens in southern Italy.

Upon learning of the treasonable conduct of his bailiff in Sicily, Emperor Sone sends one of his sons, Henri, to learn the facts of the case. The bailiff strikes Henri with a club, and for his crime he is killed on the spot. His body is then quartered and the parts are sent throughout Italy.

Sone and Odee live many years, and before they die, they see their sons advanced to high rank.

Violette

In a wager Girart loses his land to Lisiart, who through the aid of the wicked Gondree, appears to have seduced Girart's sweetheart, Euriaut. Intending to kill Euriaut, Girart instead abandons her in the forest. She is found by the Duke of Metz, who, enamored, takes her to his home in spite of her pretense at being a prostitute. There the villain Meliatir, rebuffed in his amorous advances, plots revenge. In the dark of night he murders the duke's sister, thinking her to be Euriaut, and later accuses Euriaut of the murder. In the meantime, Girart, having learned of

Lisiart's deceit, sets out in search of Euriaut. On the way he punishes Durlus, not only for wounding a man and beating his bride, but for breaking truce with the man as well. Later, at Cologne, Girart tells Aiglente, who has fallen in love with him, that he is a bad character who has forced a rich widow to marry him because he coveted her wealth. Eventually he arrives at Metz in time to prove Euriaut innocent of murder by defeating Meliatir in a judicial duel. Meliatir is immediately drawn and hanged. Together the lovers return to court, where, after the Count of Boulogne insists that nobody will have honor if there is no combat to decide the issue, Girart wins back his land and proves Lisiart guilty of treason by vanquishing him in a duel. When Lisiart has been drawn and hanged and the wicked nurse scalded to death, the lovers are happily married.

NOTES

NOTES

Chapter I

1. "Die Formalitäten des gottesgerichtlichen Zweikampfs," *Zeitschrift für romanischen Philologie,* IX (1885), 1-74.

2. Der Feuertod als Strafe, "*Studien zur englischen Philologie.*"

3. Cf. S. Barrow, *The Medieval Society Romances.*

4. A class constituting most of Miss Barrow's grouping. Faral (in Bédier and Hazard, *Histoire de la littérature française illustrée,* I, 41) says: "les romans d'aventure s'attachent à la vie réelle, la montrent, la reflétent, et pour cette raison ils s'offrent à qui veut connaitre les moeurs du XIIIe siècle comme des guides infiniment précieux. . ." The reader will observe that seven or eight romances listed are distinctly Arthurian. The fact that Langlois regards *Sone de Nansai* as a *roman d'aventure* whereas Bruce calls it an Arthurian romance reveals the difficulty of making a clear-cut classification.

5. É. Chénon, *Histoire générale du droit public et privé,* I, 557: "Son exposé, toujours très clair, révéle chez Beaumanoir un esprit net, ferme, indépendant; c'était un homme de grande valeur. On a pu l'appeler à bon droit 'le premier grand jurisconsulte françois' [Paul Gide]."

6. There is no attempt here at definitions of the terms *felon* and *felonie,* terms outside of the scope of the present study. Cf. J. Goebel, *Felony and Misdemeanor.*

7. *The Novels of Juan de Flores.* Miss Matulka's reference to the Code of Hammurabi is only a general one. Yet she should have been more familiar with more recent laws, for in note 5, p. 66, she fails, like Foerster (*Der Feuertod als Strafe,* pp. 180f.), to mention the West Gothic law stipulating death by fire for adultery, a law duly noted by Wilda (*Strafrecht der Germanen,* p. 504 and note) and corroborated by His, *Deutsches Strafrecht,* p. 141.

8. Cf. F. Gundolf, *The Mantle of Caesar,* pp. 109f.

9. Cf. chap. iv, n. 46.

10. Goebel, *Felony and Misdemeanor,* p. 187.

11. *Roman Law in Medieval Europe,* p. 69.

Chapter II

1. Regarding the organization of justice in Frankish times, see Glasson, *Angleterre,* I, 189-90, 193-95, 202, 214, 215; Chénon, *Histoire générale du droit public et privé,* I, 236-40; Goebel, *Felony and Misdemeanor,* p. 33, n. 72. For justice during the feudal period, see Chénon, *op. cit.,* I, 657-58,

661; also Beaumanoir, *Coutumes de Beauvaisis,* paragraphs 23, 24, 1883, 1920. References in Beaumanoir are always to paragraphs, not pages.

2. Although secular justice is our chief concern here, a short account of ecclesiastical justice and the influence of canon law will be helpful in getting a clearer picture of medieval justice as a whole. Out of the general scramble for increased power during the latter part of the Carolingian era, the Church, alone strongly organized, gradually widened in scope the jurisdiction of ecclesiastical courts so as to include in the twelfth and thirteenth centuries a number of crimes formerly tried in the lay courts only. The Church tribunals became popular with the laity, who, realizing the disadvantage of the risks and stringent formalities involved in secular procedure, preferred when possible the less dangerous and more sensible process prescribed by canon law. The natural repercussion was that the lay courts were forced, not only by the protests of the Church and especially by her condemnation of the barbaric ordeals but by popular opinion as well, to adopt to some degree the method of their rivals. Thus canon law based on Roman law penetrated gradually into the custumals, impregnating them with a spirit of justice and equity and at the same time obviating much of their confusion and obscurity. The nobles, however, resented the encroachments of the Church and even attempted retaliation, consenting temporarily to join forces with royalty to gain their end. The great barons were in close correspondence with Frederick II about the time of his conflict with Pope Innocent IV, and toward the end of the year 1246 they formed a confederation for the purpose of restricting the jurisdiction of the Church over the laity in cases dealing with heresy, marriage, and usury. In such contests as this, royalty was eventually the gainer since we find, for example, that adultery, heresy, and other offenses came to be regarded as royal cases in so far as they concerned the state; heresy, considered in this light, came ultimately—in the fourteenth century and much more frequently later—to be tried in royal courts only.

Although in Carolingian times erring bishops were sometimes tried in the royal court, in the twelfth and thirteenth centuries the ordinary clergy were judged for the most part in ecclesiastical courts only. This jealously guarded clerical privilege was often the cause not only of delay, but of abuse and scandal also, especially when taken advantage of by criminal laymen who sought refuge in the asylum of church or monastery, or who merely had themselves tonsured for purposes of deception. (For the material in this note the following have been consulted: Glasson, *France,* V, 164-278; Chénon, *op. cit.,* I, 269-70, 272, 280; Lea, *History of the Inquisition in the Middle Ages,* I, 221, 325; Fournier, *Les Officialités du moyen âge,* p. 101; Perrot, *Les Cas royaux,* p. 34.)

3. The etymology of this word as given by Glasson (*Angleterre,* I, 189) shows it to be apparently more Gothic than Frankish.

4. For information concerning the seneschal and other officers, see the following: Luchaire, *Histoire des institutions monarchiques,* pp. 177ff.; Glasson, *France,* V, 358ff.; Chénon, *op. cit.,* I, 575, 604, 607, 611, 615.

5. For vengeance among the Franks, see Glasson, *France*, III, 408, 420, 431, 528-32, 537, 581-83; Brissaud, *A History of French Public Law*, p. 112. And for the feudal period see Chénon, *op. cit.*, I, 687; II, 896. For the development of ecclesiastical and royal control of vengeance in the feudal period, see Chénon, *op. cit.*, I, 750-57, and Goebel, *op. cit.*, pp. 297ff. Beaumanoir is cited as the primary authority for the thirteenth century.

6. Beaumanoir, *op. cit.*, 1671-72.

7. *Ibid.*, 1673.

8. *Ibid.*, 1686.

9. *Ibid.*, 1687.

10. *Ibid.*, 887.

11. *Ibid.*, 1688-89.

12. *Ibid.*, 1683.

13. *Ibid.*, 1682.

14. *Ibid.*, 1811.

15. Cf. Luchaire, *Social France*, pp. 13f.

16. Beaumanoir, *op. cit.*, 1701.

17. *Ibid.*, 1702.

18. Cf. Bouvier, *Law Dictionary*, II, 3310.

19. See the discussion of lese majesty and treason in Lear's "The Early History of Treason," pp. 83, 146f.

20. *Ibid.*, pp. 94, 96. See also Brunner, *Deutsche Rechtsgeschichte*, (1892), II, 685ff.; and Goebel, *op. cit.*, pp. 120-21.

21. It is understood that the purely personal relationship not based on ownership of land did not cease with the advent of feudalism. Cf. Guilhiermoz, *Essai sur l'origine de la noblesse en France*, p. 236, n. 2.

22. *The Feudal Regime*, p. 40; cf. *Établissements*, II, 77, tit. LIV.

23. II, 49: "Hom quant il amble a son seignor, et il est a son pain at a son vin, il est pandables; car ce est une maniere de traison."

24. *Op. cit.*, p. 42. Cf. Beaumanoir, *op. cit.*, 1734-35.

25. Le Foyer, *Exposé du droit pénal normand*, pp. 103ff.

26. Cf. the *foi mentie* of Beaumanoir (*op. cit.*, 1772-73) and of Pierre de Fontaines (*Conseil à un ami*, ch. XXI, p. 247, section 22).

27. Page 297. Cf. Beaumanoir, *Coutumes*, 1675. Though much of the *Jostice et de plet* comes from Roman law, it is noteworthy that, according to Rapetti (Introduction, p. xii), Book XIX, in which the definition of treason occurs, owes nothing to the Digest. We may therefore conjecture that the treason defined is Germanic in principle.

28. *Établissements*, I, 76.

29. *Op. cit.*, 826-27.

30. Although a formulated conception of "malice" as we understand it appears not to have existed in Frankish times, Goebel (*op. cit.*, p. 40, n. 87) points out that the idea was expressed by such terms as *per malum ingenium, per invidiam, in inamicitiam*. While it has been said that Beaumanoir's definition of treason is wider in scope than that in the *Jostice et de plet*, it is not necessarily implied therefore that the idea of "malice" is new with

Beaumanoir, for he himself says (*op. cit.*, 6-7) that he is merely trying to preserve without change a custom which has come down from ancient times. Cf. Lévitt ("Origin of the Doctrine of *Mens Rea*"), who also indicates that the Salic Law makes no mention of the *mens rea*, but who, in speaking of treason in England says (p. 122): "Furthermore, the essence of treason from earliest times has always been intent and not the act. No harm need result from the intent or even from the acts which were treasonable. Yet punishment was imposed." To authenticate his last statement, Lévitt cites the following: Alfred 4; *Thorpe* 1, 63; Ethelstan 4; *Thorpe* 1, 203.

31. Cf. A. Tardif, *Histoire des sources du droit français*, pp. 383ff.

32. Le Foyer, *op. cit.*, p. 106.

33. *Op. cit.*, 885.

34. *Établissements*, II, 47. Beaumanoir, *op. cit.*, 1746.

35. Cf. Perrot, *op. cit.*, pp. 27ff. The term *crimen lesae regiae majestatis* appears in *Les Olim*, II, 616.

A comparison with contemporary English definitions of lese majesty not only may prove interesting but may help explain why in France the doctrine of lese majesty took a longer time to develop. The first important definition after the Conquest occurs in Glanvill's *De Legibus* (Beames, pp. 1-3; cf. Latin text, Woodbine, p. 42): The crime which in legal phrase, is termed Laese Majesty, as the death of the King, or a sedition in the Realm, or Army—the fraudulent concealment of Treasure-trove—the Plea concerning the breaking of the King's peace—Homicide—Burning—Robbery—Rape—the crime of Falsifying, and such other Pleas as are of a similar nature. These crimes are either punished capitally, or with the loss of a Member. We must, however, except the crime of Theft, which belongs to the Sheriffs of Counties, and is discussed and determined in the County Courts. It also appertains to Sheriffs, in case of neglect on the part of Lords of Franchise, to take cognizance of Scuffles, blows, and wounds, unless the Accuser subjoin to his charge, that the offense was committed against the King's Peace.

The outstanding feature of this considerable list of crimes (which strongly resembles the Pleas of the Crown detailed in the *Leges Henrici Primi* or, for that matter, the Ducal cases described later in the Norman *Summa de Legibus*) is the emphasis placed first upon injury to the person of the King or sedition against him, and second, upon breach of the King's peace. Bracton, whose great work dates from about the middle of the thirteenth century, and who usually is most copious in detail, includes under lese majesty the forging of the King's seal and the counterfeiting of his money, but omits all the other crimes mentioned in Glanvill except, of course, injury to the King and sedition against him, upon which he places great emphasis. (See Bracton, *De legibus*, pp. 257-58f.)

That one could injure the King through offense or insult to members of his family is made clear in Andrew Horne's *Mirroir de Justices*, written probably after 1290. Lese majesty is committed by those who "lie with the King's wife, the oldest legitimate daughter of the King before she be married under custody of the King; or the niece, or the aunt, the heir to the King," Whittaker's edition, p. 15. In addition to this Horne suggests the crime of heresy as a form of lese majesty not mentioned in either Glanvill or Bracton. He says that "The crime of majesty is an horrible offense done against the King; and that is either against the celestial King or the terrestrial" (*loc. cit.*).

Perhaps the most interesting account of treason is that found in *Britton*, a treatise coming after Bracton in time and generally supposed to be modeled after it:

1. Treason consists of any mischief which a man knowingly does, or procures to be done, to one to whom he pretends to be a friend. And treasons may be either great or little, of which some require judgment of death, some loss of limb, pillory, or imprisonment, and others lighter punishment according to the nature of the case.
2. Great or high treason is to compass our death or to disinherit us of our kingdom, or to falsify our seal, or to counterfeit our coin, or to clip it. A person may likewise commit great treason against others in several ways, as by procuring the death of any one who trusts him; as for instance those who poison their lords or others, and those who lead persons into such perils, that they lose life and member or chattels.
3. The judgment in high treason is to be drawn and to suffer death for felony. The same judgment is incurred by those, who in appeals of felony are attainted of having counterfeited or otherwise falsified the seal of their lord, of whose dependence or homage they are, or of adultery with the wives of their lords, or of violation of the daughters of their lords or the nurses of their children. And if a woman be attainted of treason, let her be burnt.
4. Where persons are attainted of crimes of this nature at our suit, let them be sentenced for falsifying a seal, if the act be of small consequence, to the judgment of pillory only, or to lose an ear; but if the act be of importance and heinous, as touching disherision or lasting damage, they shall be judged to death. And of other offence let Holy Church have correction (I, 40).

Besides being the first important English treatise after the Conquest to be written in French instead of Latin, *Britton* is not only the first to drop the term *lese majesty* in favor of the expression "high treason," but is, furthermore, the first to include a definition of "little" or petty treason. Upon closer examination, however, petty treason as described in *Britton* seems to differ little from high treason except in scope and in the condition that it does not apply to the injury of royalty. The first sentence of the complete definition in *Britton* sharply distinguishes it from the definitions given in both Glanvill and Bracton, and shows a strong similarity to those in the thirteenth century French custumals, especially Beaumanoir's. In *Britton* both high and petty treasons are merely species of the genus treason—treason in general, which is briefly described as treachery to the person to whom one pretends to be a friend. The general emphasis on lese majesty in all English definitions, however, is not lightly to be passed over. The English conception of treason after the Conquest, whether influenced more by Roman law, as seems likely, or by Germanic law, developed under the sanction and guidance of royal authority. From William the Conqueror on, English kings had assumed complete control of a strongly centralized government; and the works of Glanvill and Bracton applied to all England, not simply to a feudal division of it. As we have already seen, different political conditions in France naturally brought about different results.

36. *Op. cit.*, 992, 997. Cf. also the corresponding chapters on *tricherie* in Pierre de Fontaines and the *Jostice et de plet*. The general idea of treachery, malice, evil, etc., was often loosely described in the earlier *chansons de geste* by the term *felony*, which by the end of the twelfth century had acquired a technical meaning in feudal law in France; it indicated a breach of faith by a man against his lord. We may conjecture that as the thirteenth century advanced, the term *treason*, particularly in the romances, came to be used in a general sense very much as the word *felony* had been used. It is clear from the custumals that *treason* is a word used to describe the wicked state of mind of a man committing, or about to commit, a major crime. There is some similarity between Beaumanoir's definition of treason and the English statute of 1352 (25 Edward III, Statute 5), according to which an act is not even necessary to constitute treason. See S. Rezneck's article, "Constructive Treason by Words in the Fifteenth Century," *American Historical Review*, April, 1928, which clarifies some of the confusion about the interpretation of parts of the 1352 statute.

37. Regarding the phase of Frankish procedure thus far discussed, see Glasson, *France*, III, 403, 420, 428, 429.

38. *Ibid.*, 433-34.

39. Page 52, section lxv: Li pledeeur [men of law] souloient metre en merci les simples homes, qui sanz le commandement a la justice s'agenolloient a fere leur seremenz, e quant il ooient quc il estoient acusé de ce que s'estoient agenollié, si se levoient e li pledeeur les acusoient derechief de ce que il s'estoient levé sanz la commandement a la jostice, e einssi les escrivoit li clers en merci. De ce dist Normanz d'Ogiervile que il avoit tant vescu que il veoit joer en la cort le roi a Bernart le Beccant, si comme li emfant joent e dient: "Or sus, Bernart," e se il ne se levast maintenant, il fust tainz de charbon en la face, autresi taignoit li clers en son parchemin les simples en merci.

40. Bar, *History of Continental Criminal Law*, p. 177.

41. Beaumanoir, *op. cit.*, 1154, 1908.

42. *Ibid.*, 174.

43. *Ibid.*, 178.

44. *Ibid.*, 182.

45. *Ibid.*, 180, 183.

46. *History of Continental Criminal Procedure*, p. 11.

47. *Ibid.*

48. II, 187, 407. Cf. below, n. 74.

49. See Goebel, *op. cit.*, pp. 326-27.

50. See Goebel, *op. cit.*, p. 42, n. 93. Contrast this with Roman procedure, which, though essentially accusatory in nature, was less formal, made use of written court records, interpreted evidence more reasonably, and utilized methods of proof which were practiced by the accuser, not the accused, and which were affirmative rather than negative in principle (Esmein, *op cit.*, p. 18; Brissaud, *op. cit.*, p. 117, n. 3). But cf. Beaumanoir, *op. cit.*, 1192. For Roman influence in general, see Vinogradoff, *Roman Law in Medieval Europe*, chapter on France.

51. *Op. cit.*, 1163.

52. As it was, there did arise later a school of legal hairsplitters known as the Bartolists, of the kind later satirized by Rabelais and concerning whom Glasson (*France*, IV, 220) quotes the following amusing criticism: "Verbosi in re facili, in difficili muti, in angusta diffusi."

53. *Op. cit.*, 934.

54. Glasson, *France*, III, 406, 408; Esmein, *op. cit.*, p. 61.

55. Beaumanoir, *op. cit.*, 1570, 1571.

56. The proof by witness did not occur often in the Merovingian period since most of the early laws authorized it only in rare cases, generally such as the attesting of a permanent fact known to all the community. Sometimes in this period witnesses themselves were duped, if we may credit the following story told by Gregory of Tours in his *History of the Franks* (II, 155). According to the tale, a certain Andarchius, enamored of a girl, gave her mother his mail shirt in a case, telling her that there were more than 16,000 gold pieces in it, whereupon she promised him the daughter. Andarchius then got a royal order from the king and came back with it to get the girl, but Ursus, her father, said he knew nothing of him or his claim.

A quarrel began, and as it increased in vehemence, Andarchius demanded that Ursus should appear with him before the king. But when he had come to the royal villa of Berny, he fetched another man named Ursus, whom he brought privily to the altar, and made to swear in the following words: "By this hallowed place, and by the relics of the blessed martyrs, I swear that if I give thee not my daughter in marriage, I will repay thee sixteen thousand pieces of gold." Now witnesses were standing in the sacristy, listening unobserved to what he said, but unable to see who it was that spoke.

When the proof by witness was used at all in the Carolingian era, it was unsatisfactory for various reasons. The parties involved could choose their own witnesses. A litigant had the right to object to the deposition of his opponent's witness and provoke the latter to a judicial duel—a proceeding which, as Lea says (*Superstition and Force*, p. 120), adjourned the main case and decided its result. If the witnesses disagreed, whether they were of the opposing parties or of the same party, they settled their difference only by resorting to the duel (Glasson, *France*, III, 489-90; but cf. Beaumanoir, *op. cit.*, 1761). Testimony was often perjured and unreliable, especially if the witnesses had been drinking (Chénon, *op. cit.*, I, 253). During the eighth century proof by witness fell into a disrepute which, prolonging the use of judgments of God, lasted until the thirteenth century, when the *Établissements de Saint Louis* insisted upon the deposition of witnesses in place of the judicial duel (II, 8). According to Beaumanoir, however, this mode of proof had changed little and in fact retained nearly all of the features described above (1170ff. Also chap. xl). In most cases women and clerics were not allowed to testify because they could not have the wager of battle; bastards and serfs were heard only under limited conditions, while lepers and criminals were denied deposition altogether (1174-77, 1185, 212). A litigant who was in a position to accuse his opponent's witness of some crime profited therefore by at least a temporary advantage. On a debated question no pleader could have less than two witnesses or more than ten, and though a party proved his point with three witnesses, the opponent might win the decision if he proved his point with four witnesses (1257).

57. Proof by presumption was probably influenced considerably by canon law. Cf. Fournier, *Les officialités du moyen âge*, p. 200-201. In canon law there were four grades of presumption: *temeraria, probabilis, violenta,* and *necessaria.*

58. *Op. cit.*, 1156.

59. *Ibid.*, 1158.

60. *Ibid.*, 942, 939.

61. *Ibid.*, 1815.

62. G. Baist, "Der gerichtliche Zweikampf, nach seinem Ursprung und im Rolandslied," *Romanische Forschungen,* V, pp. 444ff. See also Chénon, *op. cit.*, I, 672.

63. Gregory of Tours, *History of the Franks,* II, 334-35.

64. Chap. lxxxiv, 1.

65. *Les Olim,* II, 165 (arret de 1280).

66. *Superstition and Force,* p. 77.

67. Cf. Goebel, *op. cit.*, p. 121, n. 203.

68. *Superstition and Force,* p. 101-2.

69. *Chivalry,* p. 34.

70. Lea (*Superstition and Force,* p. 137) gives the following reference: Innoc. PP. iii. Regest. VI 26 (c. 2 Extra, v. 35).

71. Beaumanoir, *op. cit.*, 1840.

72. Cf. *ibid.*, 1721.

73. *Établissements de Saint Louis,* II. 323; cf. Beaumanoir, *op. cit.*, 1810, 1795, 1796, 1800-1801.

74. Beaumanoir, *op. cit.*, 1841. Cf. above, n. 48.

75. *Ibid.*, 1721.

76. Lea, *Superstition and Force,* pp. 234-35.

77. See S. Grelewski, *La Réaction contre les ordalies en France depuis le IX° siècle jusqu'au décret de Gratien.*

78. Another reason for their use, the incredibility of the suspect's oath, is noted by Goebel, *op. cit.*, p. 322, n. 121.

79. *Très ancien coutumier de Normandie,* XXXIX and XXXIX bis.

80. Lea, *Superstition and Force,* p. 319.

81. *Ibid.*, p. 288.

82. *Ibid.*, p. 408. Lea quotes the following prescription by Albertus Magnus: mallow and radish juice, white of egg, lime, and psillus seeds.

83. *France*, VI, 646-47.

84. K. von Amira, *Die germanischen Todesstrafen*, chap. ix, "Die sakraler Charakter der öffentlichen Todesstrafe." His, *Strafrecht bis zur Karolina*, p. 56.

85. His, *op. cit.*, p. 56.

86. *Germania*, 19.

87. His, *op. cit.*, p. 141; *Lex Visigothorum*, III, 4, 2.

88. His, *op. cit.*, p. 149; *Lex Burgundionum*, Tit. lii.

89. His, *op. cit.*, p. 141.

90. *Ibid.*, pp. 74-75.

91. *Ibid.*

92. *Ibid.*

93. *Ibid.*

94. Bar, *op. cit.*, p. 109.

95. Page 278.

96. *Op. cit.*, 14: La tierce vertus que li baillis doit avoir, si est qu'il doit estre dous et debonaires, sans felonie et sans cruauté; et non pas debonaires entre les felons, n'envers les crueus, n'envers ceux qui font les mesfès, car a teus manieres de gens doit il moustrer semblant de cruauté et de felonie et de force de justice, pour leur malice estre mendre. Car tout aussi comme li mires qui le malade, pour pitié de sa maladie, lesse a ateindre la plaie de laquele il le doit garir, le met en peril de mort, tout aussi li baillis, qui est debonaires vers les mesfesans de sa baillie, met ceus qui vuelent vivre en pes en peril de mort; ne nus plus grans biens, uns pour un, ne puet estre a baillif que d'essarter les mauvès hors des bons par radeur de justice. Donques ce que nous avons dit qu'il doit estre debonaires, nous l'entendons vers ceus qui bien vuelent et vers le commun pueple, et es cas qui avienent plus par mescheance que par malice. Et pour ce que nous avons dit que sapience est la souveraine vertus de celes qui doivent estre en baillif, l'en ne doit pas tenir le baillif pour sage qui vers tous est fel et crueus. Et souvent avient que les simples gent, qui ont bonnes quereles et loiaus, lessent perdre leur quereles pour ce qu'il ne les osent maintenir par devant teus baillis pour leur felonie, pour doute de plus perdre.

97. *Les Olim*, I, 135. J. R. Strayer, *The Administration of Normandy*, p. 23. Cf. also Langlois, *Le Regne de Philippe III le Hardi*, p. 30.

98. *Op. cit.*, 16.

99. Beaumanoir, *op. cit.*, 839, 840, 844, 865. Cf. also Goebel, *op. cit.*, p. 241.

100. C. L. Tanon, *Histoire des justices*, pp. 330, 332. The fact that death was often the punishment for a third offense may have accounted for the end of the man who stole the egg.

101. His, *op. cit.*, p. 75.

102. Huizinga, *The Waning of the Middle Ages*, p. 16.

103. See above, n. 39 and 40. For an extended account of *misericordia*, see Goebel, *op. cit.*, pp. 242ff.

104. Glasson, *France*, V, 274.

105. Although Beaumanoir was not favorable to the *lex talionis* (841), he did speak frequently of public vengeance or the vengeance of society (823ff.).

106. Glasson, *France*, V, 274.

107. Cf. Gelzer, in his edition of *Yder*, p. cii: "Philipp II Augustus kann auch nicht in Betracht kommen. Er hat sich in 1193 nach langer Witwerschaft mit Ingeborg von Dänemark verheiratet, verstiesse sie aber bald darauf und vermählte sich mit Agnes von Meran. Durch Intervention des Papstes Innocenz III wurde er gezwungen, seine Ehe mit Agnes für ungültig zu erklären, behielt sie aber als Geliebte bei. Erst lange nach ihrem Tode nahm er 1213 Ingeborg als Gemahlin an."

108. Chénon, *op. cit.*, I, 278f.; Goebel, *op. cit.*, p. 225, n. 73.

109. E. van Cauwenbergh, *Les Pélèrinages expiatoires et judiciaires dans le droit communal de la Belgique au moyen âge*, pp. 8, 23, 29, 30, 161.

110. See below, pp. 46, 49-50; also p. 91.

Chapter III

1. Beaumanoir, *Coutumes*, 312.
2. Car ele est mescreans et fole,
   De deu ne vuet oir parole,
   Mariage het et despise
   Et sacrement de sainte glise. (ll. 12885-88)
3. Se il nos dist mencونge u voir. (l. 13978)
4. Por les mescreans justicier / Et por la loi deu avancier. (ll. 14149-50)
5. "Sire," dist il, "de voir sachies,
   Que tant est de mavaise loi
   La roine que je ci voi,
   Qu'ele ne doit terre tenir . . .
   (ll. 14284-87)
   Doi je par jugement avoir . . .
   (l. 14292)
   Pres sui de mostrer or endroit,
   C'on le doit essilier par droit,
   Et puis c'om le set si meffaite,
   Elle doit estre arse . . ."
   (ll. 14299-302)
6. Ce sachent bien li archevesque / Et li abe et li evesque. . . (ll. 14333-34).
7. Et chevalier et clerc et lai (l. 14387).
8. Kate Norgate, *England under the Angevin Kings*, II, 96.
9. *Ibid.*, II, 98.
10. Z. N. Brooke, *The English Church and the Papacy*, pp. 216-17. Stubbs, *Constitutional History of England*, I, 310, 503. Maitland, "Henry II and the Criminous Clerks," *Collected Papers*, II, pp. 233, 236.
11. Goebel, *Felony and Misdemeanor*, p. 168.
12. *Ibid.*, p. 310, n. 86; p. 317.
13. *Chronicle of the Crusades*, translated by Marzials, pp. 151, 305. Cf. *Histoire de Saint Louis*, de Wailly, XIII and CXXXV, pp. 23, 241.
14. H. C. Lea, *History of the Inquisition in the Middle Ages*, I, 221, 325.
15. *Ibid.*, I, 191.
16. Beaumanoir, *Coutumes*, 341.

17. See below, pp. 71-72.
18. Lines 5627ff.
19. Lines 696-704.
20. Glasson, *Angleterre,* I, 258.
21. Esmein, *Cours élémentaire d'histoire du droit français,* p. 359.
22. Introduction, pp. v-vi.
23. Lines 6794-95.
24. Line 6824. Although the term *accort du roi* as used here may mean simply the advice or consent of the king (cf. below, n. 191), there may be in it a reminiscence of the early Frankish term *sermo regis,* which implied special protection by the king (Goebel, *op. cit.,* p. 49). The opposite term, *extra sermonem regis,* might possibly be applied to the wicked aunt, who refuses to come to the king's court when summoned, for Goebel (*op. cit.,* p. 52) says: "In the *Lex Salica* itself, where the expression *extra sermonem* occurs it is a part of the final process against a defendant who refuses attendance at the king's court." It is probable that the term *forbannitus* is even more appropriate to the wicked aunt, for in Carolingian law the person against whom the foreban is directed may be seized by anyone; moreover, the foreban carries with it a ban upon property, the *missio in bannum,* which amounts to confiscation of property if, within a year and a day, it is not redeemed through fulfillment of the obligation previously refused (Goebel, *op. cit.,* pp. 112-13).
25. Par raison et selonc droiture / Sanz peril et sanz forffecture (ll. 6827-28).
26. Lines 6870-75.
27. Que le conte par son lignage, / Par sez homes et par sa force, / La praigne . . . (ll. 6928-30).
28. Li roys a la forfecteüre / De mon cors et toute ma terre (ll. 7628-29).
29. Lines 6928ff.
30. Grant conseil assemble / Et sez grans barons tous ensemble (ll. 7713-4). The description of the king's court just given calls to mind a remark made by Gautier ("L'Idée politique dans les chansons de geste," *Revue des questions historiques,* VII, 95) concerning royal courts in the *chansons de geste*—a remark which may possibly assist the reader in forming a better picture of royal courts in the romances, particularly in *Comte d'Anjou:*

Les trouvères écrivaient, après tout, dans un temps ou le Conseil du roi était véritablement organisé. Nos derniers poètes virent même cette révolution importante par laquelle les anciennes commissions provisoires du Conseil devinrent le Parlement et la chambre des comptes. Il n'est donc pas étonnant que le souvenir des anciennes Assemblées nationales se soit un peu mêlé et confondu dans leur esprit avec la notion du Conseil du roi, tel qu'il fonctionnait des les XII° et XIII° siècles.

C'est dans nos plus vielles Chansons que l'on trouve la plus exacte de ressemblance entre les Conseils tenus par Charlemagne et les Champs de mai carolingiens. Dans les uns commes dans les autres, les conseillers n'ont qu'une autorité toute consultative: non-seulement le pouvoir éxécutif, mais la decision elle-même appartient à l'Empereur.

Although Maillart was well acquainted with the royal court as it was in 1316, when he wrote the *Comte d'Anjou,* there was nothing to prevent him, since he was writing fiction, from harking back to Carolingian times for a model. Yet his court is slightly different; the king, whose every decision is made only after advice from his counsellors, appears not quite so independent in action as the Carolingian emperor.

31. Li roys molt volentiers le gree
Et li donne la forfecture,
Car il en est hoir par droiture, . . .
(ll. 7750-52)

32. Lines 7773ff.

33. See p. 19.

34. *Coutumes,* 1669: li rois . . . puet contraindre les parties a fere pes ou a donner trives . . . et meismement quant guerre muet entre ceus qui sont du lignage, li sires doit metre mout grant peine a la guerre oster, car autrement puet estre li lignages destruis pour ce que chascuns en la guerre seroit par devers son plus prochien, dont il avient a la fois que li uns cousins tue l'autre.

35. *Ibid.,* 85: il convient bien que li ajournés viegne a son ajournement, ou il seroit en defaute. Car puis qu'ajournemens es fes . . . les parties ne le pueent pas delessier sans la volenté du seigneur. Ainçois convient que cil qui a fet fere l'ajournement poursieve ce seur quoi il l'a fet ajourner; . . . Et s'il le poursuit et li ajournés se defaut, il doit estre justiciés pour les defautes; et s'il en i a .III., il est atains du fet seur lequel il fu ajournés.

36. Chénon *op. cit.,* II, 225.

37. See p. 14.

38. Of the romances under discussion the *Comte d'Anjou* offers the nearest approach to an ecclesiastical court. When the Count of Bourges after a long search at last finds his wife and child, the almoner of the church where the countess has accepted charity informs the bishop in order that "leur afaire encerchera" (l. 5986). Since all cases pertaining to marriage came under the jurisdiction of the church courts (see Beaumanoir, *Coutumes,* 313), it is therefore within the bishop's province to investigate the relations between the young couple. But his inquiry seems to be an informal one, and there is no mention of court procedure or of other ecclesiastical officers, for "Tout sa gent fet en suz traire, Lez deus retient tant seulement Et leur encerche doucement" (ll. 6046-48). The informality of the inquiry is increased when the bishop discovers that the young countess is his niece (l. 6250).

39. Il ot traÿ la gent (l. 20256).

40. Lines 20252-336.

41. Perrot, *Les Cas royaux,* p. 27.

42. Henri qui voloit justichier (l. 20325).

43. *Op. cit.,* p. 30.

44. Lines 4433-48.

45. Introduction, p. lxxiii.

46. See Chapter II, n. 34, and Perrot, *op. cit.*, p. 76, Bris d'asseurement royale.

47. Lines 5538-49.

48. Tu en morras! Prenez le moi! (l. 5733).

49. Tu me prendras? Mes je preng toi. / N'es tu mes hom? (l. 5734).

50. Donc t'apeau je de traïson! (l. 5736).

51. "Belchis, vos estes soz;
Contre lui a mout poi des voz
Ceenz se traïtor ne sont.
Bien sachent cil qui mesferont
A mon seignor cui hom je sui,
Que mes pooirs est devers lui
Contre vos se meslee i sort.
Vos meïsmes en vostre cort
Me feïstes le serement
Jurer; sachiez certainement
Que je l tendrai."
(ll. 5747-57)

52. Lines 3797-5797.

53. Chénon, *op. cit.*, II, 147.

54. Gawain says: je jurrai ainz / Fëauté voianz toz sor sainz / Vos ederai contre toz homes (ll. 5531-33). According to the *Summa* (XXVII) the oath is as follows: Ego devenio homo vester ad portandum vobis fidem contra omnes, salva fidelitate ducis Normannie.

55. Cf. *Summa de legibus*, XXVII, 5: Fit autem homagium quandoque de pace servanda, quod homagium de paga nominatur, eo quod fit in pagam concordie inter aliquos reformate, ut quando aliquis sequitur alium de aliqua actione criminali et pax inter ipsos reformatur, ita quod secutus facit homagium alteri de pace illa conservanda; hujusmodi homagium recipitur in pagam concordie reformate. Cf. also R. His, "Totschlagsühne und Mannschaft," p. 366. See also Mitteis, *Lehnrecht und Staatsgewalt*, pp. 484f.

56. Meraugis says: Qu'il n'est riens nee qui me plese / Fors li, ne terre ne avoir (l. 5780-81). The poet says: Meraugis a la dame, / Mes a la terre a il failli (ll. 5796-97).

57. "Nos serions / Parjure se nos alion / Contre lui" (ll. 5761-63).

58. Page 290.

59. *Op. cit.*, 825. Simple homicide Beaumanoir describes as occurring when "aucuns tue autrui en chaude mellee, si comme il avient que tençons nest et de la tençon vient laide parole et de la laide parole la mellee par laquele aucuns reçoit mort souventes fois" (828).

60. I, 235f.; II, 37-38.

61. Line 222.

62. Lines 218-340.

63. Line 4009.

64. Lines 3994-4031.

65. Line 6342.

66. Lines 5725-68.

67. Line 2346.

68. Line 15928.

69. Line 531.

70. La l'ocistrent desloiaument, / Car traitre sont desleaux / Et envers toz preudomes faux (ll. 9841-43).

71. ". . . l'autre jor ocist mon pere
Et puis apres andeus mes freres;
Si m'a trencié et char et cuir
Et tant m'a fait que je me muir.
Par les plaies me saut l'alaine,
Et avoec lue m'amie enmaine.
Pis m'est-il de sa deshonor
Que il ne soit de ma dolor.
Il est repus en .i. buisson;
Si me feri en traïson,
Si que jou venir nel vi mie."
(ll. 221-31)

72. *Op. cit.*, 327: Li secons cas de quoi sainte Eglise ne garantist pas celui qui en est coupables, si est de celi qui est notoirement roberes en chemins en aguet apensé; car quant il est suis de tel fet et il fuit a garant en lieu saint, li lieus ne garantist pas que la justice ne le puist prendre et justicier comme larron et traiteur.

73. Line 3402.

74. Lines 3254ff.

75. Line 3302. Cf. Luchaire, *Social France*, pp. 8ff.

76. *Op. cit.*, 992: Et se vilains fes avint par la tricherie, pour lequel cas li feseur doivent recevoir mort, cil par qui tricherie ce fut fet, en doit porter autel peine comme cil qui le firent, car poi de disference a entre tricheeur et traiteur. Car li tricheres veut couvrir sa tricherie souvent avient par beles paroles et souvent avient qu'il la pourchace si traitrement et si malicieusement que l'en ne puet avoir tesmoins contre li.

77. Line 3214.

78. Line 3977.

79. Line 6987.

80. Line 13714.

81. Line 13709.

82. *Coutumes*, 1099: Mes la ou tele fraude pourroit estre trouvee, li bareteeur qui font la fraude et tuit li consentant doivent estre pugni comme larron.

In England, however, according to Glasson (*Angleterre*, III, 587-88) this crime would have been considered an indirect form of lese majesty.

83. Line 14635.

84. Line 261.

85. Lines 520ff.

86. Line 412.

87. Cf. chap. ii, n. 53.

88. Line 960.

89. *Coutumes*, 934.

90. See below, n. 210.

91. Cf. chap. ii, n. 88.

92. Lines 3206-7.

93. Je l'ocirai a mes .ij. mains (l. 3825).

94. Line 3378.

95. Lear, *Early History of Treason*, p. 3.

96. Bar, *op. cit.*, p. 102.

97. H. Euler (*Recht und Staat in den Romanen von Christian von Troyes*, p. 85) points out that adultery is regarded as treason in *Charette*, l. 4874, *Cligés*, ll. 6631f., and *Erec*, l. 3469.

98. Lines 4402-11.

99. *Coutumes*, 925.

100. Lines 1603-6, 5653f.

101. "Frere," fet il, "trop grant otrage
Fait gentis hom de grant parage,
Qui fame esforce voirement; . . .
(ll. 24053-55)
Car trop i a grant mesprison
Et cruiaute et traison,
Car feme ne se puet defendre,
Car par nature est mole et tendre
Et li hons fiers et durs et fors; . . .
(ll. 24059-63)

102. Tanon, *Histoire des justices*, pp. 417-18, 426. Adultery in England was a form of petty treason.

103. Lines 23842-61.

104. Lines 9396-98.

105. Lines 705-9.

106. "Mais dites moi, ne vos anuit / U vos presistes ces deus cies. . ." (ll. 836-37).

107. Dalton's translation, II, 387f.

108. *Wort und Form im altfranzösischen Process*, pp. 674f.

109. Comfort's translation, p. 263; Foerster, *Löwenritter*, ll. 6384-98.

110. Cf. Beaumanoir, *Coutumes*, 1748: Il est mestiers a celui qui veut apeler autrui ou pluseurs persones d'aucun vilain cas de crime qu'il se gart comment il apelera; car s'il en veut apeler .II. ou .III. ou plus, et il les veut tous metre en gages, il doit apeler l'un tant seulement en sa persone et doit avoir presentement de ses amis pour apeler les autres, si que chascuns en apeaut un; car s'il les apeloit tous en sa persone et il s'offroient tuit a defendre, il convenroit qu'il se combatist tous seus a tous ceus qu'il avroit apelés, et de cel cas veismes nous ce qui ensuit en la court le roi.

111. Comfort, *loc. cit.*, p. 228; Foerster, *op. cit.*, ll. 3674-87.

112. The term *avocat* occurs once, without reference to any individual, in the *Comte d'Anjou*, l. 3483. Delachenal ("De l'avocat dans la littérature du moyen âge") and Meynial ("Remarques sur la réaction populaire contre l'invasion du droit romain en France au XIIe et au XIIIe siècles") deal more with the satirical literature and sermons than with the romances.

113. Comfort, *loc. cit.*, p. 332; Foerster, *Der Karrenritter:* "Je sai de causes et de lois / Et de plez et de jugemanz: / Ne doit estre sanz seiremanz / Bataille de tel mescreance" (ll. 4964-67).

114. *Rigomer*, ll. 1529-1808. Beaumanoir, *Coutumes*, 971: Une fame qui tient en douaire, se l'en la despueille de son douaire, se puet bien plaindre de nouvele dessaisine, tout soit ce contre l'oir a qui la chose venroit se la fame estoit morte, car il n'i a riens tant comme elle vive.

115. From the reference in note 113 we have already seen that Lancelot is particular about the oath before battle. Likewise in the *Erle of Toulouse*, fearful of perjuring himself in the oath before battle, the earl "examyned hur wytterly" and found the queen "wythowte gylte" (ll. 1063f.).

116. Line 886.

117. Cf. Beaumanoir, *Coutumes*, 934, 1188, 1189, 1637.

118. Line 4522.

119. Car mes sires le veult tuer (l. 4696).

120. Line 485.

121. To the one who has read both the *Châtelain de Coucy* and the *Comte de Poitiers* the evidence of marital infidelity in the former is more convincing than that in the latter. In *Comte de Poitiers*, however, the court accepts the false evidence (see p. 73 of this chapter) and puts the Duke of Normandy in the dangerous position of having admitted the equivalent of betraying the count's wife. Had the count in vengeance slain the duke, even as he had sought vengeance against his own wife, he might by a little cleverness have got off scot-free, for Beaumanoir (*Coutumes*, 932) tells of a like situation that occurred during the reign of Philip Augustus. A man who had killed another because the latter had said, "You are cuckolded, and by me myself," put himself in the king's prison and confessed the deed, saying that in seeking justice he had killed the other as his enemy since the latter had proved himself one by taunting him of so great a shame. The man was freed by judgment of Philip and his counsellors. It appears then, in spite of what Beaumanoir has said elsewhere, that in a case of adultery the husband may in some circumstances kill a man not actually found in flagrant delinquency. Such a possibility, however, does not apply to the Sire de Fayel, for his retainer, Gobert, may act as a witness against him instead of for him. Fayel's caution is therefore completely justified.

122. "Jugement et loi li voel faire, / Sans jugement nel voel desfaire" (ll. 5362-3). Cf. Beaumanoir, *Coutumes*, 46.

123. "Cele qui fu el fait trouvee
Fu en tel point prise prouvee,
Que le coutiel encor tenoit,
Dont le puciele occise avoit;
Et encor est teus li recors
Qu'ele avoit le coutel el cors,
Si que cele tenoit le manche;
Et qui ne diroit par esmanche,
Puis que trouvee est en tel ghise,
Que cele ne l'eüst occise?
Li fais et la veüe prove
Que qui onques en tel point trove
Il n'i a bataille ne loy.
A cest parolle m'aloy
C'on le doit par droit jugement
Ardoir et livrer a torment; . . ."
(ll. 5388-5403)

124. "Li hom qui jugement emprent
Fait mal quant il i entreprent;
Que pechiés est de dire tort
Ne de traitier nului a mort,
S'on n'i set loiel ochoison.
Bien avés oï la raison
Que dist li sires de Lansi,
Que elle fu trouvee ensi
Qu'encore tenoit le coutiel,
K'Ismayne avoit sos le forciel
Desci au manche enbatu ens.
Je di, teus est mes escïens,
Que, se cele l'eüst ferue,
Ele s'en fust tantost courue.
Cuidiés qu'elle s'i endormist?
Certes, onques ne s'entremist
De faire si grant hardement;
On peut savoir legierement
Que s'ele s'en fust entremise,
Lués se fust a la voie mise;
Mais elle fu dormant trouvee.
Sachiés, c'est verités prouvee,

K'en dormant ne le feri mie;
Et si sai bien, je ne douc mie,
Se feru l'eüst en villant,
Je m'alaisse molt mervillant,
Se ne s'en fuïst orendroit.
Jouste la loy, si di le droit,
C'on voist a li et demant on
Se ele a fait cest murdre ou non.
S'ele dist non, Meliatir,
Que j'oï orains aatir,
Prenge l'escu et le baston,
Car elle a ja son campïon;
Et si me faich de chou confiés
C'on devroit miex sor lui le fais
Metre de ceste oevre, je cuit;
Et Dex la puciele en acuit,
S'ele encoupee n'en doit estre."
(ll. 5426-64)

One may readily believe that Sire d'Aspremont knows more of pleas and laws than any other knight in the world, for we may find interesting a comparison of parts of his speech with passages from Beaumanoir. Although Beaumanoir is speaking of rape and abduction while Sire d'Aspremont is concerned with a case of murder, the similarity in phrasing is indeed noteworthy. Compare lines 5426-30 with the following in the *Coutumes* (929): grant pechié fet la justice qui reçoit gages en cas ou il ne doivent pas estre, car il metent les parties en peril de perdre cors et avoir.

And compare lines 5453-59 with the following, also in the *Coutumes* (929): Et s'il semble a la justice qu'ele responde assés as demandes qui li sont fetes et que ce puist bien estre voirs, li gage sont a recevoir.

125. Beaumanoir, *Coutumes*, 836.

126. In the treatment of the episode just discussed, Gerbert exhibits a greater knowledge of the law than the author of *Florence de Rome*, whose heroine, in a situation similar to Euriaut's, escapes death not through the clever argument of any judge, but through the boundless mercy of the man whose daughter she is suspected of having murdered (II, 196, ll. 4772ff.). For other heroines in like predicaments see Schlauch, *Chaucer's Constance and Accused Queens*, p. 112.

127. Cou dist Pepins: "Par St. Denise
Jà n'en sera juise prise.
Li Franc dient à recélée
Vos ensagnes vous ont provée; . . .
(ll. 428-31)
Cil vous dechut par legerie,
S'ara Poitau et Normendie,
Et vous arés poverte et honte.
(ll. 438-40)

128. Lines 972-977.

129. Lines 3575-5079.

130. Page xviii, n. 2.

131. Si vos di, s'ele fust as lois
V ans toz plains sanz removoir,
Ce sachiez de fi et de voir,
Je ne sai por coi ne coment
Ele peüst plus belement
Son claim dire ne son afere.
(ll. 4754-9)

Beaumanoir says (*Coutumes*, 190) that a woman could not act as an *avocat* for payment, but without payment she could speak for herself, for her children, or for anyone of her kin, with the consent of her husband, if she had one.

132. Beaumanoir says (*Coutumes*, 991): L'en ne doit pas oïr toutes persons en plet de tricherie. Car se li fius veut pledier a son pere ou a sa mere en

aus metant sus tricherie; ou li serjans a son seigneur tant comme il est en son service; ou li hons de fief a celui a qui il est hons tant comme il est en son homage; ou li sires contre le franc homme; ou li escommenié; ou li parjure, ou cil qui sont ataint de vilain cas de crime, tout soit ce qu'il en fissent pes, contre persones qui sont delivres de tous teus cas; ou cil qui sont disfamé contre ceus qui sont de bonne renomee: toutes teus manieres de gens ne sont pas a oïr en plet de tricherie, li un pour ce qu'il sont en si vilain point qu'il semble que il meisme soient en l'estat de tricherie, et li autre pour les obeïssances qu'il doivent a leur peres et a leur meres et a leur seigneurs.

The capitulary referred to is 1 *Cap.* 334 c. 8, cited in Goebel, *op. cit.*, p. 260, n. 151: "in palatiis nostris ad accusandum et iudicandum et testimonium faciendum non se exhibeant viles personae et infames, histriones scilicet nugatores, manzeres [de scorta nati] scurrae, concubinarii, neque exturpium feminarum commixtione progeniti aut servi aut criminosi."

133. Cf. p. 32.

134. Paragraph 1, p. 37.

135. Paragraph 2, p. 37.

136. A few examples of ordeals not occurring in the group of romances under discussion are as follows: In *Tristan* (Chap. xxiv, pp. 210-11) Ysolt, by means of the ambiguous oath, successfully performs the hot iron ordeal. The ordeal by fire occurs in the Middle English romance, *Athelston* (ll. 568-end): a whole family pass over the fire unscathed, but the false accuser collapses on the way over. In "Guthrunarkvitha" III (*Poetic Edda*) Guthrun successfully performs the hot water ordeal, but her accuser does not. Similar ordeals occur in Caesarius of Heisterbach's *The Dialogue on Miracles,* I, 40; III, 16, 17; X, 35. Alwin Schultz (*Das höfische Leben,* II, 175) notes the occurrence of the bier-right in the romance *Walewain,* ll. 8826f.; the dead man's wounds bleed afresh as the murderer draws near. Perhaps the earliest mention in the romances of this superstition appears in Chrétien's *Yvain* (ll. 1175-85); under the cloak of invisibility Yvain causes the wounds of Laudine's husband, fatally injured in the battle at the fountain, to bleed afresh.

137. Li juïses fu luès tot prest
Au moustier mon segnor S. Pierre
Qui ert coverz de fuelle[s] d'ierre.
Tuit i vienent, prince et demaine,
Et li seneschauls q'en amaine;
Et la pucele vint ovoeques,
Par le conseil des arcevesques,
Por veoir la bone droiture.
A grant honte, par sa ceinture,
Fu li senescgaus esgardez.
Luès droit qu'il fu laienz entrez,
En l'eve qui estoit segniée,
Lues droit plus tost q'une coignée,
S'en vet au fons trestoz li cors
Si que la bele Lïenors
Vit qu'il fu sauz, et tuit li autre
Qui furent d'une part et d'autre
Entor la cuve atropelé.
Li clerc en ont mout Deu loé
En lor chanz et en sains soner.
(ll. 4982-5001)

138. Fuller accounts of judicial duels in the romances will be found in

Pfeffer's "Die Formalitäten des gottesgerichtlichen Zweikampfs," *Zeitschrift für romanischen Philologie,* IX (1885), 1-74, and in G. Schoepperle's *Tristan and Isolt,* II, 338ff.

139. Cf. O. Leibecke, *Der verabredete Zweikampf, passim.* A. Dickson (*Valentine and Orson,* p. 79 n.) adds to Leibecke's list. Other forms of treachery and deceit in the judicial duel not in the romances discussed in the present study are as follows: In *Parise la Duchesse* (ll. 276-602) a traitor offers to defend Parise and then, by previous arrangement, yields himself recreant. In *Amis et Amilun* (ll. 493ff.), because of the resemblance between the two heroes, Amilun substitutes for Amis (who is involved in a suit), takes an ambiguous oath before battle, and defeats Amis's opponent. Sometimes a powerful champion disgraced the cause of righteousness; in *Eustace le moine* (ll. 304-371) Hainfroi, over sixty years of age and accused of murdering Eustace's father, hires a great hardy vassal who in the duel immediately kills the young and inexperienced nephew of the murdered man.

140. Lines 254ff. Cf. A. Coulin, *Der gerichtliche Zweikampf.*

141. Cf. Joinville, "Everyman's," p. 263 (p. 182 in de Wailly). Cf. also *Les Assises de Jerusalem,* II, Chap. cxxv and cclxix.

142. Lines 3593-3676.

143. See Beaumanoir, *Coutumes,* 824, 830, 831, 832, 833, 834; *Établissements de Saint Louis,* II, 46, 48, 51, 79; *Jostice et de plet,* pp. 279ff.

144. R. His, *Das Strafrecht des deutschen Mittelalters* (I, p. 495, n. 6): Die früheste Stelle in einem Gesetz ist soviel ich sehe, Keure des Domänenamts Antwerpen, 1292. A. Schultz, *Höfisches Leben,* II, p. 180, n. 3; p. 182, n. 1; p. 183, n. 1. Miss K. Huganir ("Equine Quartering in *The Owl and the Nightingale,*" *PMLA,* December, 1937, pp. 935ff.) implies not only that equine quartering was common in the twelfth century, but also that at the same time the infliction of this penalty for the crime of lese majesty was the "highest prerogative" (p. 944) of the king. If it was the highest prerogative of the king, it would hardly have been exercised in all "the law courts of the twelfth century" (p. 943); consequently the statement that the *Owl* poet "must have known equine quartering at first hand" (p. 943) seems doubtful. Furthermore, if the infliction of equine quartering was the highest prerogative of the king, we should suppose it to be important enough to get into historical records, but Miss Huganir cites none. In fact, in presenting historical examples of equine quartering itself, she skips from the Edonians to the seventeenth century, omitting the twelfth century altogether, although Schultz (*op. cit.,* II, 180, n. 3) quotes Ordericus Vitalis (Lib. VIII, cap. xxii), who records an example of equine quartering in Scotland in the year 1125. But even here Prévost, editor of Orderic's work, points out (III, 403, n. 1) that, though there is little reason for disbelieving this account, it is not mentioned by any of the contemporary Scottish historians.

145. Glasson, *Angleterre,* III, 600.

146. Glasson, *France,* VI, 695. See below, n. 152.

147. Henris qui voloit justichier
A fait le baillieu depechier,
En quatre quartiers fu partis.
Atelés a .IIII. ronchis.
Li uns est a Trapes alés.
Li uns des trois qui sont remés,
A on viers Rise a voie mis,
Et li tiers en va a Brandis,
Li quars en va en Lombardie.
Or a Henris la car partie.
La puet on exemple moustrer,
Comment on doit des faus ouvrer.
(ll. 20325-36)

148. Baist, cited in W. Foerster's "Der Feuertod als Strafe," p. 181.

149. L. Gautier, *Les Épopées françaises,* I, 30.

150. J. Grimm, *Deutsche Rechtsalterthümer,* II, 272f., K. von Amira, *Die germanischen Todesstrafen,* pp. 131f.

151. Grimm, *ibid.* DuCange, *Glossarium mediae et infimae latinitatis,* V, 551.

152. *Coutumes et institutions de l'Anjou et du Maine,* II, 502.

153. Viollet, *Établissements,* I, 183.

154. *Ibid.,* II, 46-47.

155. Le Foyer, *op. cit.,* p. 183.

156. Lines 4528ff.

157. Jonas, li roi de Taubarie,
S'est trais avant; premiers parla:
"Seignor, fet-il, entendez, çà.
Voirs est Maragoz est outrez;
Mès il estoit rois couronnez.
N'est pas raisons que on l'ocie:
Rois ne doit pas perdre la vie.
Certes, se nous le jugions,
Grant vilonie ferions;
Et si vous di bien vraiement,
Chascuns ne set qu'à l'ueil li pent.
Tiex hons a jà jugié autrui,
Qui puis en ot honte et anui,
Qu'en tel fet méismes cheoit
Et ses jugemenz l'ocioit:
Pour tant diroie, sanz fausser,
C'on le devroit laissier aler."
Rois Brangoire est avant passez:
"Seignors, fet-il, or m'entendez.
Dès que Maragoz est vaincuz,
Et par sa bouche est connéuz
Li murdres qu'il méismes dist,
Que son lige seignor ocist,
Roiauté n'i doit riens valoir.
En ma raison vos di por voir
Que on li doit le chief coper;
Je n'i puis autre riens trover."
Roi Natalons passa avant,
Qui le cors avoit avenant:
"Seignors, fet-il, entendez-moi;
Je dirai verité . . .
(ll. 5644-74)
Por tant lo bien laissier l'ester
Rois Maragoz, par tel couvent
Qu'il vous jurera erraument
Que jamais, tant com il vivra,
En ceste terre n'enterra."
Rois Bande [ma] gus s'est dreciez,
Qui moult estoit bien enseigniez:
"Biaus seignors, fet-il, entendez . . .
(ll. 5690-97)
Maragoz ocit son seignor . . .
(l. 5703)
. . . en traïson;
Si ot trop grande mesprison.
Por tant loeroie endroit moi
Que on l'ardist, foi que vous doi."
Après parla li rois Turcanz,
Qui hardis ert et combatanz:
"Seignors, fet-il, or m'entendez,
Li rois Maragoz est outrez
Et connoist bien la traïson;
Mès ne me samble pas raison

Qu'il soit ocis, au mien espoir.
Rois ne doit pas mort recevoir
Pour riens qu'il sache meserrer.
Faisons-le em prison geter:
C'est li plus biaux, ce m'est avis." . . .
Rois Uriens en piez se drece,
Qui moult ert plains de grant noblece:
"Seignors, fet-il, entendez çà:
Selonc mon avis vous dira.
Dès que Maragoz est outrez
Et par .j. chevalier matez,
Et il connoist la traïson,
N'i voi riens se de la mort non.
Or le faisons en mer geter,
Une grante pierre au col noer;
Em poi d'eure sera noiez:
C'est li mieudres que vous sachiez."
Après parla rois Geremie,
Qui estoit sires de Hongrie:
"Seignors . . .
(ll. 5707-36)
Je n'i voi riens del eschaper,
S'el face-on au vent encroer."
Loth, li riches rois d'Orcanie,
Qui onques n'ama vilonnie,
Mesdisant ne losengeor,
Ne desloial ne traïtor,
S'est maintenant dreciez em piez:
"Biaus seignors, fet-il, or m'oiez.
Maragoz son seignor ocist,
Dont trop grant desloiauté fist,
Et puis après desherita
Sa dame, et après l'aseja
En Monreal com traïtour;
Puis ala à l'empereour,
S'el fist venir en ceste terre.
Bien sunt ocis de ceste guerre
.X. mil chevalier esprouvé;
Par lui seul sunt tuit decolé,
Quar par lui seul mut l'achoison.
(ll. 5742-60)

158. Adonc fu Maragoz mandez,
Et par les .ii. piez acouplez;
Parmi l'ost le vont traïnant,
Une ore arrier et autre avant,
Tant qu'il fu trestous despeciez.
.iiij. vallez fors et haitiez
Vont après, s'ont les pieces prises
Et toutes en .j. moncel mises.
Li rois fist .j. gibet drecier;
Tantost fist, sanz plus atargier,
Les pieces pendre maintenant,
Ensi doit-on felon tirant
Destruire et mener à sa fin.
(ll. 5796-5807)

159. von Amira, *Die germanischen Todesstrafen*, p. 190; beheading was the most honorable execution: see His, *Deutsches Strafrecht*, p. 82. Cf. *Cléomadés*, ll. 3910-20:

Par gentillece I don vous ruis,
C'est que vous pas ne me pendez
Comme larron qui est prouvez;
Car les chevaliers ne doit on
Pas pendre, s'il ne sont larron,
Ou s'il n'ont par trayson fait,
Murdre ou autre vilain mesfait.
Et, puis c'ocire me voulez,
J'aim miex estre tous decoupez
D'espées et de dars molus
K'estre comme larres pendus.

The sentencing of King John is discussed in Powicke's *The Loss of Normandy*, Appendix I, pp. 453ff. A more recent discussion appears in Mitteis's *"Politische Prozesse des früheren Mittelalters,"* pp. 84ff.

160. Brunner, *Rechtsgeschichte*, II (1928 ed.), 818, 820; G. Waitz, *Verfassungsgeschichte*, VI, 482; His, *Strafrecht*, I, 537, 558.

161. *Op. cit.*, p. 197, n. 1.

162. *Ibid.*, pp. 194, 142.

163. Meliatir fait atachier
A la keue d'une jument,
Trahiner le fait molt vilment
Dusch'a forches, puis pendirent.
(ll. 5639-42)

164. Glasson, *France*, I, 120; Chénon, *op. cit.*, I, 6.

165. Mes l'en li met sus, qu'ele a mort
Son mari, qu'a fame l'avoit,
Chevalerie assez avoit.
L'autrier la dame se leva,
Son mari lez soi mort trouva,
Qui lez li gisoit en son lit,
Dont au cuer ot pou de delit . . .
La nouvele fu tost alee,
Que li chevaliers estoit morz,
S'en fu molt granz li desconfors
Communement par le pais,
Car il ert des meillors nais.
Quant ses freres sot la nouvele,
Sachiez, ne li fu mie bele!
Forment le plaint et regreta
Et puis sa femme en apela;
Sus li mist, qu'ele mort l'avoit.
Cele dist, que nianz estoit
Et qu'onques pense ne l'avoit
Et qu'ele s'en defenderoit
Par l'esfort d'un seul chevalier . . .
(ll. 9683-9704)

166. Pages 817, 820. Alton refers to ll. 37768ff.

167. "Everyman's," p. 121. I have interpolated the word *burn* since the Latin (Lib. VI, XIX) says: ". . . et si compertum est, igni atque omnibus tormentis excruciatas interficiunt."

168. Lines 6366-94.

169. Nul droit ne. l poet de mort defendre, / Que l'om deit bien traïtor pendre; / Temoine i ont de plosors pars (ll. 3137-39).

170. Cf. *Les Olim,* I, 41 (arret de 1258), 737 (arret de 1268), and 830 (arret de 1270).

171. Lines 16052-85.

172. Lines 711-13.

173. Line 352.

174. Cf. Luchaire, *Social France,* pp. 8ff.

175. Et li visquens est adrechiés / Vers lor maison, ardoir le fait / Et le mur ont par terre trait (ll. 1042-44).

176. II, 38, 248; see also Delcourt, *La Vengeance, passim.*

177. Section 25, p. 280: Li avocaz qui par lor gloriose voiz relièvent les causes qui sunt abessies, se il font tricherie ès causes que il ont à mener, il soffreront poine de traïson. Cf. also *loc. cit.*, 26: "Lit notenier, li taverner, li ostelier, se il ne gardent ce que il recevront en cez trois lieus, et il facent tricherie, il recevront paine de traitor." See *loc. cit.*, 27.

178. Lines 14105-6.

179. *Coutumes,* 832.

180. Lines 4545-53.

181. *Social France,* p. 356.

182. Lines 6132-59.

183. His, *Strafrecht,* I, 563; Grimm, *Rechtsalterthümer,* II, 276.

184. A preliminary to the wicked aunt's final punishment is her ignominious ride from prison to the scene of the execution in a cart. In this connection one naturally recalls Lancelot's humiliation and what

Chrétien de Troyes has to say on the subject of carts: "In those days such a cart served the same purpose as does a pillory now; . . . and this, like our pillories, had to do service for all those who commit murder or treason, and those who are guilty of any delinquency, and for thieves who have stolen others' property or have forcibly seized it on the roads. Whoever was convicted of any crime was placed upon a cart and dragged through all the streets, and he lost henceforth all his legal rights, and was never afterward heard, honored, or welcomed in any court." (Comfort, *loc. cit.*, p. 274; ll. 323-340.) That Chrétien was speaking of a contemporary rather than an ancient custom as far as the cart itself was concerned may be verified from an incident which, according to Luchaire *(Social France,* pp. 303-04), occurred about the year 1204: "Peter of Courçon . . . was detested by the clergy, because they knew it was he who had advised and incited the Count [Peter of Courtenay] in the war he had waged against the church. For a long time Hugh of Noyers [the bishop] could not injure this man, because he was protected by the favor of his master. But there came a day when Peter of Courçon fell into disgrace, and the bishop of Auxerre hastened to profit by it. He had him arrested, put him in a cart with four wheels, and had him conveyed chained and bareheaded (he was absolutely bald) through all the streets and squares of Auxerre; he was followed by a hooting crowd."

185. Li un jugent que toute vive
Soit escorchie la chetive
Huy ung membre, l'autre demain,
Tant qu'il n'y ait ne pié ne main
Qu'escorchié ne soit salé;
Et puis le corps soit avalé
En une orde privee obscure:
C'est a luy digne sepulture.
Les autres dïent que l'en l'arde,
Mes tout avant que l'en la larde
De goutes de saïn ardant.
Li tiers dient . . .
(ll. 7779-90)
Face la a cevaus detraire
Et tous lez membres du cors traire,
Et puis la lesse au chienz mengier:
. . .
Et dit li dus . . .
"Fac'en li quens ce qu'il voudra,
Car d'une mort seule mourra."
. . .
Dit li quens, fectes la mener
Sous le gibet et amener
Des espines a grant foison:
Si li brulerons sa toison
Et li ferons ardoir en cendre!"
A la prison vont sanz actendre.
Hors la traient par l'eschelete;
Mise l'ont en unne charete,
Au feu s'en vont droite la voie
Mez criature qui la voie
Ne la plaint ne pitié n'en a
Tant mal en son temps se mena
Vers ceus qui souzgis li estoient
. . .
(ll. 7793-7817)
La fist li quens u feu geter;
Et elle fu estroit lïee,
Si fu tantost toute embrasee,
Car li feus estoit grans et fors.
Au desreignier par grant esfors
Geta un bret let et orrible;
Deable . . .
L'ame de li en enfer portent.
(ll. 7848-56)

186. See p. 37.

187. Godefroy de Paris, *Chronique métrique*, ll. 6222ff.

Por leur traïson et péchié,
Qu'il furent vif escorchié;
Puis fu lor nature copée,
Aux chiens et aux bestes jetée,
Et puis traîné et pendu.
(ll. 6292-96)

188. Cf. Perrot, *op. cit.*, p. 27.

189. His, *Strafrecht*, I, p. 502. von Amira, *op. cit.*, p. 196.

190. Line 575.

191. *Coutumes*. 1718, 1846.

192. *Ibid.*, 1718.

193. For early times see H. Wegele, *Zur Geschichte der falschen Anschuldigung*, p. 15; cf. Delattre, *Recherches sur le droit pénal à Cambrai*, p. 137. For the 14th century see Glasson, *France*, VI, 675.

194. See above, pp. 29, 35.

195. Comfort, p. 239; Foerster, ll. 4570-75. Cf. Thomas Aquinas, *Summa theologica*, Part II (Second Part, second number) Q. 68, Art. 4.

196. Lines 1128-30.

197. *Comte de Poitiers*, l. 1219; *Violette*, ll. 6560-63.

198. Lines 5569ff. Similarly in *La Châtelaine de Vergi*, the duke, who kills his wife because in breaking a promise she has disobeyed him, takes the Cross and joins the Knights Templar, never again to return to his own land. Cf. van Cauwenbergh, *op. cit.*, p. 25: In 1264 four murderers agreed to go to the holy land to fight in the crusades and never return unless authorized to do so by the victims' families. Cf. also the penance incurred by Robert in *Robert le Diable* (ll. 839-907), who after having committed such crimes as arson, rape, and murder, repents, makes a pilgrimage to Rome, and learns from a holy man designated by the pope that, until directed otherwise, he must simulate a fool, must not utter a word, and must eat nothing except what he takes from a dog's mouth. We may find a rough parallel to this penance in Luchaire's *Social France*, p. 305: "In 1219, Gilles, lord of Saint-Michel in Laon, rid himself in the same way of the abbot of Saint-Michel, with whom he was at war. The murder was committed in the very cloister, and he who had planned it was barely fifteen years old. He promised, first, to go and fight the Albigenses; then to make a pilgrimage to Rome, where the pope would inflict penance upon him; every Friday, for fourteen years, he was to eat nothing but bread and water; he was to support three paupers, if he could not fast; three times a year, on a day of solemn procession, he was to discipline himself publicly; and he was to establish in perpetuity in the abbey of Saint-Michel a priest to pray for the soul of his victim."

199. Beaumanoir, *Coutumes*, 824, 926; *Assises de Jerusalem*, II, ch. cxxxiv, cxxxv; His, *Deutsches Strafrecht*, p. 145; His, *Strafrecht*, p. 494, n. 9.

200. Brunner, *Rechtsgeschichte* (1928) II, 859; Mayer-Homberg, *Die frankischen Volksrechte im Mittelalter*, I, 308; 308, n. 48.

201. Lines 292-95, 352. Car il voloit sa volenté/Faire de li . . . (ll. 292-3).

202. Qui cuidoit bien pierdre la uie/V la tieste avoir rouengnie (ll. 409-10).

203. Lines 5653ff. Crompart dies in prison because, upon alighting near Salerno with Clarmondine in order to rest, he refuses to answer questions put to him by King Meniadus, who is very fond of news from the outside world, and who

Lors jura sa loi erranment
Que, se tost et apertement
Ne dit ce que il li demande,
Que soufrir angoisse très grande
Li fera, et enprisonner,
Et telement enchaienner,
Que à tart s'en repentiroit
Se il de lui plus se mokoit.
(ll. 6987-94)

Such a curious law as this, though perhaps Celtic, scarcely belongs to the Middle Ages. It is possible, however, that like the author of *Claris et Laris*, Adenet le Roi was also a close reader of the *De bello Gallico*, for Caesar describes as follows a custom prevalent among the Gauls; "it is the custom of that people to compel travelers to stop, even against their inclination, and inquire what they may have heard, or may know, respecting any matter. . . ." ("Everyman's," p. 67; Lib. IV, V).

204. See ll. 4388-4428, 8002-30. Although it is doubtful whether according to Adenet a man's own country would be likely to punish him for treason he committed in another land, the details given about the exile are generally correct, particularly those concerning the formalities required at the criminal's return, for van Cauwenbergh says (*op. cit.*, p. 166):
Avant de réadmettre le condamné dans la commune, les autorités voulaient avoir de sérieuses guaranties au sujet de l'accomplissement de la peine imposée; elles exigeaient qu'il vint presenter le certificat de voyage et faire le serment de l'authenticité de cet acte comme de l'observation complet des points stipulés dans sa condemnation. Si la voyage avait été prononcé en faveur d'une partie lésée, le tribunal convoquait en même temps celle-ci pour lui déclarer que le condamné ayant satisfait à ses obligations, la paix était retablié antre eux. Si la partie adverse ne comparaissait pas, les juges proclamaient neanmoins le condamné "en paix dele voye."

205. According to von Amira (*op. cit.*, p. 191), stoning was chiefly a punishment for theft.

206. *Les Olim*, I, 815. In Tournai the seven-year exile was imposed for the abduction of a married woman—an offense similar to Crompart's: Quicumque uxorem alicujus hominis infra civitatem manentis abduxerit, inbannitus civitatem per septem annos relinquat; si postea reconciliatus redeat, res illius hominis quas cum muliere asportavit, ex integro ei restituat (Usus & consuetudinis Tornacensis [year 1187], III, 552. in J. L. d'Achery, *Spicilegium*).

207. On le devroit delivrement/Descirer a .IIII. chevaux/Et par les monz et par les vaux (ll. 24056-8).

208. Glasson, *France*, VI, 662.

209. See the closing episode of *Joufrois*, beginning about l. 4000.

210. Cf. p. 63 of this chapter; Brunner, *Rechtsgeschichte* (1928) II, 850, 851, n. 6.

211. Lines 3952-54.

212. In early times adulteresses had their hair cut off (Grimm, *op. cit.*, II, 287). DuCange (*op. cit.*, II, 137) quotes a mid-fourteenth century source to show that the shorn head indicates a fool. But in *Meraugis de Portlesguez*, written not long before 1215, the heroine does not at first recognize Meraugis, who is convalescing incognito at the castle of Belchis, because his head is shorn: Il ne li faut fors la maçue/A sembler fol le plus a droit /Dou mont (ll. 4946-48). And in *Amadas et Ydoine* the hero, temporarily deranged, in poor garments and with hair cut, is hooted at by the mob in the city of Lucca (ll. 2724-28).

213. II, 24-25.

214. Lines 514-15.

215. Lines 6564-71. Grimm (*op. cit.*, II, 285) points out that this punishment was considered a "turpe supplicium."

216. Lines 1220-24.

217. His, *Deutsches Strafrecht*, p. 152, and His, *Strafrecht*, I, 520.

218. Viollet, *Établissements*, I, 243; II, 48.

219. See above, p. 38.

220. Vous estes repris à ambler,/Vassal, l'oreille avez perdue (l. 5399f.).

221. Gautier d'Arras: Las! ques peciés m'a ecombré (l. 1713). The word *peciés* could very well be translated here as *misfortune* or *calamity*, as it is in the *Chanson de Roland*, ll. 15 and 3646. But Marsile, the Saracen king, in uttering the expression, "Quels pecchiez nos encombret!" refers to the invasion of the Christian hosts under Charlemagne, not to the loss of a part of his anatomy. While Ille certainly may be said to consider himself unfortunate in losing an eye, he may also have in mind the idea of sin, for according to an early capitulary (see above, n. 218) the loss of an eye branded a man as a thief. Cf. also n. 220.

222. *History of English Law*, II, 498. In early times what was almost as bad as the loss of an eye or an ear was the cutting off of the hair or beard (cf. above, n. 212 and Grimm, *op. cit.*, II, 285). Like Ille in *Ille et Galeron*, the seneschal in the *chanson de geste Floovant* suffers an accident (ll. 63ff.), but one which in this day of clean-shaven faces seems more amusing than serious. The king's son, young Floovant, has just peeled himself an apple, and with the paring knife he thoughtlessly cuts off the old seneschal's long white beard while the noble is enjoying an after-dinner nap in the garden. Only the greatest self-control prevents the seneschal from taking the boy's life then and there, and it is only through the intercession of the queen that King Clovis exiles Floovant for seven years instead of having him put to death. Out of deference to the seneschal and to mitigate his disgrace, Clovis and all his barons shave off their beards. Cf. also *Gui de Bourgogne*, ll. 14-51.

223. See *Établissements*, II, 498.

224. Qui n'ait tous ses membres (l. 798).

225. Espoir qu'ele a la main colpee
Par son mesfait, est envoïe
Seule par mer sans compaignie.
Par son mesfet? Ce ne peut estre.
(ll. 1550-53)

226. "une esgaree,/Une chaitive, une avolee,/Une femme o tout une main" (ll. 2059-61).

227. "Espoir que on li a retrait/La ou il est, dont ele est nee,/Et pour coi eut la main colpee" (ll. 3536-8).

Chapter IV

1. G. B. Fundenberg, *Feudal France in the French Epic*, p. 85.
2. See above, p. 16.
3. *The Feudal Regime*, p. 65.
4. See chap. ii. n. 16.
5. La s'assist par desous un orme
Li rois, entour lui ot maint homme.
La commenchent a recorder
Se il poroient acorder
Les deus barons sans cop ferir . . .
"Che ne sera mie conqueste
Au roi, tres bein le vous creant,
Se l'uns fait l'autre recreant;
Mais qui poroit biele pais faire
Et ceste bataille desfaire,
Che seroit la plus biele fins."
Ensi va disant li daufins.
"Par foi, dist li quens de Bouloigne,
Tel parole n'est fors aloigne,
Que il n'i a nule raison.
Cist l'apiele de trahison,
Et chascuns a oï l'apiel.
Je n'iere ja par mon chapiel,
En liu que jou puisse savoir,
Pour pramesse ne pour avoir
La ou trahisons soit couverte,
Ains ert seüe et aouverte;
Que li escripture tiesmoigne,
Si le nous dïent clerc et moigne
Que chou est li plus lais pechiés
Dont nus hom puist estre entechiés,
Que de demener trahison.
Or entendés autre raison
Que la divinités recorde:
Ki orendroit feroit l'acorde
Et Gerart sa terre rendroit,
Si vous di jou trestout por droit
Que pour chou ne seroit estainte
La renomee dont atainte
Fu Eurïaus et decaüe;
Et si rest bien chose seüe:
Qui de trahison est retés
Que puis en est tous jors doutés.
Par cest point ne puis jou savoir
Que nus i puist hounour avoir,
Se il font pais, se Dex me salt!"
(ll. 6305-47)

6. It is not likely that the Vulgate uses the word *treason* in the sense meant by the Count of Boulogne (Cf. Michael Bechis, *Repertorium Biblicum Totius Sacrae Scripturae Concordantiae*, under *proditio* and *traditio*); nor so far as I have been able to discover does what the Count of Boulogne say about the making of peace and about Euriaut's ill fame correspond to anything in Thomas Aquinas's *Summa*.

7. But had Girart in the beginning been less thoughtful of his own honor, he might have saved Euriaut considerable humiliation. Professor W. W.

Lawrence (*Shakespeare's Problem Comedies,* p. 191) remarks: "It is noteworthy that the King does not attempt to dissuade the hero from accepting the wager, since he could not in honor refuse to take it up. Instead, the king endeavors to influence the villain Lisiars not to press it. But Girars, the perfect knight and lover, cannot allow any suspicion of faithlessness to rest upon his lady, and calls for the immediate binding of the contract." Girart's initial attitude and his subsequent stubbornness therefore seem to corroborate Briffault's remark (see n. 8, below) that honor "contained nothing that was inconsistent with . . . what we should account a degrading lack of self respect"; in Girart's case at least it was consistent with what we should call little or no respect for Euriaut.

8. *The Mothers,* III, 399. For other conceptions of honor see R. P. Kettner, *Der Ehrbegriff.* Cf. also Goebel, *op. cit.*, p. 151.

9. *Social France,* p. 366.

10. Mais bien te di, gariz seroit/Li leirres qui enbler l'en poroit (ll. 826-27).

11. "Wherefore the husband who exercises this kind of control over his wife may not kill her, but he may accuse or chastise her in some other way" (*Summa theologica,* Part III, Supplement, p. 284, Q. 60, Art. 1, Reply Obj. 4). The index to Albertus Magnus's *Liber de mulieri forte* (p. 218) suggests beating: "Poenae sive flagella dantur a Deo docem modis, et non sunt simpliciter malum." The chapter referred to (III, 1) does not, however, use the word *flagella* at all.

12. *Coutumes,* 1631: car il loit bien a l'homme a batre sa fame sans mort et sans mehaing, quant ele le mesfet, si comme quant ele est en voie de fere folie de son cors, ou quant ele desment son mari ou maudit, ou quant ele ne veut obeïr a ses resnables commandemens que preudefame doit fere. . . .

13. Philippe de Mousket, *Chronique rimée,* ll. 16900f. Quoted in Fundenberg, *op. cit.*, p. 39.

14. Nevertheless one example occurs in the *High History of the Holy Grail* (*Perlesvaus,* "Everyman's,," p. 49; Nitze and Jenkins, I, 76): He mounteth his horse and taketh his shield and his spear, and maketh the lady to be taken of the dwarf by her tresses and maketh her to be led before him into the forest. And he bideth above a pool where was a spring, and maketh her enter into the water that flowed forth full cold, and gathereth saplings in the forest for rods and beginneth to smite and beat her across upon her back and her breast in such sort that the stream from the spring was all bloody therewithal. [Later (p. 50) the jealous husband kills his wife by running a spear through her.]

15. Lines 302ff.

16. Car li trahitres l'ot jus mise
Trestoute nue en sa chemise
L'ot fate li fel despoillier
Si le tiennent troi chevalier
Par les bras molt estroitement,
Et il molt angoussousement
Le batoit d'un rain d'aiglentier
Si qu'il ne laissoit entier
Cuir sour le char se molt poi non.
(ll. 4485-93)

17. Li Castelains en fu irés,
De ses gans le fiert sor le nés:
Sa bouce et ses mentons rougi
Del sanc qui jus en respandi.
(ll. 990-3)

Cf. Chrétien's *Erec* (Comfort's translation) pp. 14, 63.

18. Je suis une fole esgaree
Essillie et mal eüree . . .
. . . se vous saviés mon afaire,
Anchois me feriiés desfaire,
Enfouir ou ardoit en fu; . . .
Il ot trois ans en cest esté
Que je devinc femme legiere,
Et sui apielee Ligiere,
Et sui fille a un caretier;
Encor servi d'autre mestier,
Car un larron fossier sivoie,
Qui de vair, de gris et de soie
Me vestoit, k'il aloit enblant;
Et il m'amoit au mien samblant
Plus que nule autre creature,
Tant qu'il avint par aventure
Que ceste robe que j'ai chi
Embla l'autre soir a Couchi.
Porsivi fumes longhement,
Tant que par un espiement
Fu pris, et je sui eschappee,
Ki bien deüsse estre encoupee.
N'avés de tel femme mestier.
Recommenchier voel mon mes-
tier.
(ll. 1161-1216)

19. *Coutumes,* 226.

20. *Summa theologica,* Part II, Q. 10, Art. 4, p. 96. A lie which in its very nature is hardly jocose but nevertheless not contrary to charity, and in which the good of one's neighbor is the apparent intention occurs in *Amadas et Ydoine,* ll. 5116ff. Ydoine, though married to a man she cannot love, has kept herself virgin for Amadas, whom she does love. Having come under a magic spell and believing herself about to die, she tries to prevent Amadas from suffering grief at her death by telling him that she is not only not a virgin, but that she has had of her three cousins three infants, all of whom she has murdered with her own hands.

21. *Summa theologica,* Part II, Q. 10, Art. 4, p. 96.

22. Par Diu, ma dame,
Jou reubrai l'autr'ier une fame
Qui de grant avoir estoit riche;
Baron avoit eüt trop niche,
Un chevalier riche et escars.
Son avoir ne traisist un cars,
K'il avoit ensamble aüné.
Molt cuidai bien avoir finé,
Que la dame une nuit ravi
Pour l'avoir que jou encovi.
A moillier le pris et a per.
Quant ele me pot eschaper,
A la justiche se clama;
Ensi la terre tolu m'a.
Poi sui poissans n'i os aler.
(ll. 3274-87)

Cf. Beaumanoir, *Coutumes,* 926: mes s'ele disoit que force li fust fete et disoit la force fete et comment, et que pour paour de mort ele obeï a sa volenté et, si tost comme ele peut, ele se mist hors de son pouoir pour estre a sauveté, adonques i seroient li gage pour la reson du rat.

Cf. also *ibid.,* 929: Mes s'ele dit: . . . "Il amena un prestre en secré lieu qui m'espousa et je ne l'osai veer qu'il ne m'ocisist," elle respont assés quant a cele demande.

23. *Coutumes,* 956: Pour ce, se je tieng la chose ou vueil esploitier de laquele j'avrai esté an et jour en saisine pesiblement, et on la m'oste de ma main ou de la main a mon commandement, ou l'en me veut oster la chose

a grant plenté de gent ou a armes, si que je n'i ose estre pour paour de mort, en tel cas ai je bonne action de moi plaindre de force et de nouvele dessaisine. Vous poués veoir que nule tele force n'est sans nouvele dessaisine, mais nouvele dessaisine est bien sans force, si comme il est dit dessus.

24. "Vos me rendrés cel cheval noir,
Car a mon frere le reubastes
Et en mëisme le navrastes . . .
Le fil a mon cousin germain
Et se li trencastes le main.
Pruec vos apiel de felonie."
(ll. 4880-85)

25. "Vassal," fait il, "par mesprison
M'avés reté de traison;
Mais pres sui que jou me desfenge,
S'il est qui les gages prende,
Tout ensi con cil juceront
Qui a jucier nos averont."
(ll. 4893-98)

26. *Coutumes,* 985: Male chose seroit, se l'en me toloit mon cheval ou vouloit tolir, et je avoie pouoir du rescourre, se je ne le pouoie rescourre sans estre justiciés de la justice. Mes se la force n'est pas moie, si qu'il m'est tolus et en est li toleres en saisine, je ne le doi pas aler retolir, mes arester le puis fere par justice et moi plaindre de la toute. Et se li chevaus est conneus a miens, il me doit estre rendus,—ou se je le preuve,—ne l'en ne doit nus gages recevoir en tel cas, car se li toleur et li robeur pouoient venir a gages de leur mesfés, il s'ameroient mieus a combatre qu'a estre pendu sans bataille, pour esperance d'eschaper; et male chose seroit qu'il me convenist combatre pour mon cheval qu'il m'avroit esté tolus et que l'en savroit communement qu'il seroit miens. Nepourquant cil a qui je metroie sus la toute pourroit alliguier tel cause et estre de si bonne renomee que, seur la preuve de la cause qu'il alligueroit, pourroient cheoir li gage: si comme s'il me metoit sus que je li eusse vendu ou donné pour son service ou presté, et je ne pouoie la toute prouver et je li nioie le don, le prest ou la vente, bien en pourroit venir a gages. Et tout autel que nous avons dit du cheval entendons nous des outres choses tolues ou esforcies.

27. "Sire," fait il, "le jucement
Vos dirai jou assés briément:
Il en sera faite une jouste,
Car je ne voel que il plus coste.
S'il vos abat del cheval noir,
Il le devra quite ravoir,
Et se vos del sien l'abatés,
Le noir tout cuite retenés."
(ll. 4901-8)

28. *Op. cit.,* p. 216.

29. *Ibid.,* pp. 142-43.

30. G'iere dame d'une abaie
Qu'ore est durement esbahie,
Car uns chevaliers destruit l'a
Et dit, que ses aieus y a
Donne du sien si largement,
Qu'encor l'en est pis voirement;
Si veut prendre ses mengeries,
Ses sejours et ses beveries;
Li chevaliers est forment riches,
Mes trop par est avers et chiches
Et de l'autrui terre prenanz
Et vers toutes genz mesprenanz."
(ll. 27004-15)

31. Cf. also ll. 26985-89.

32. "hault baron de sa terre/Qui plus obaïr ne vouloit/A li, si con faire souloit" (ll. 3094-96).

33. *Circa* ll. 1000ff.

34. *Op. cit.*, pp. 4, 260, 286, 290. Cf. also Delcourt, *La Vengeance*.

35. Lors est en I pais entres
U il a devant lui trovees
Les viles arses et gastees,
Fortereces voit abatues
Et glises arses et fondues,
Les molins trueve depecies
Et les jardins tos essilies.
. . . .
Mais tot ainsi cum il erra
Plus de VII C homes trova
Sor le chemin sanglens et mors,
Trestot nu gisoient li cors,
Si n'estoient pas mis en terre;
Bien senbloit, qu'iluec eust guerre.
Li pais ert si destorbes
Et si malement desertes,
Qu'en vint liues en I tenant
N'ot home ne fame manant.
(ll. 10414-34)

The fact that the bodies were naked is evidence of the plundering that usually went on after a battle.

36. For an account of ambush, see *Les Olim*, I, 41; for breaking of *assecuracionem* and for beating (eum verberavit), see *ibid.*, I, 450, IX, and also 737, 830.

37. Viollet in *Établissements*, I, 232-33.

38. "Ueber absichtlose Missethat," p. 488.

39. *Coutumes*, 887: Nepourquant l'en puet bien metre a mort autrui en tel maniere que l'en n'en pert ne vie ne membre ne le sien, en deux manieres: la premiere si est quant guerre est aouverte entre gentius hommes et aucuns ocist son anemi hors de trives et d'assurement; la seconde maniere si est de tuer autrui seur soi defendant.

40. Jean Boca, *La Justice criminelle*, p. 268, cites the *Livre Rouge* as follows: En l'an de grace mil CCC LXX IIII, le XXIVe jour de juillet, environ heure de vespres sonnant à Saint Ulfran, advint que un nommé Robert d'Espaigne, sueur, ala assalir asses près de le Bare as quevaulx u quemin, Nicaise Thibergue, un coutel tout nu en se main. Li quels Nicaise saca se badelaire et se mist à deffence et navra ledit Robert telement que mort s'en ensievy incontinent en la pièche si comme par boins tesmoins fut sceu, et ossi confessa ledit Nicaise, en présence du maïeur et eschevins, le XXVe jour dudit mois, après che que le mort li fu monstré, que che que ledit Robert avoit, che avoit esté par li, et que che li avoit il fait sans che que se femme lui fust en riens aidans ne confortans à che faire; et pour che, par le maire et eschevins fu ledit Nicaise jugié à rechepvoir mort; est assavoir de estre trainés et pendus; et fu ledit jour exécuté as fourques de le ville d'Abbeville.

41. "Vassal, vassal, ja comperrés/Le damage que fait m'avés/De mon neveu que avés mort" (ll. 2237-39).

42. "Vos avés tort/Assés aim mix, foi que vos doi,/Que je l'aie mort que il moi,/Et sor moi deffendant le fis" (ll. 2240-43).

43. Regardé ont vers un pendant;
Mener l'en voient tot batant:
Comme larron l'en amenoient
Les mains loiies li avoient
Et ambesdex bendés les iex.
(ll. 2277-81)

44. Compare this question with the question King Arthur asks of the cruel damsel who has disinherited her sister (p. 67).

45. Au mestre dit: "Vous renderes
Le mal mourdrier que vous aves.
Le roy no signour nous mourdri.
Car en traÿson le feri."
Dist li templiers: "Ce ne savons.
Un chevalier chaijens avons.
Toutes les coses nous rendres
Et apriés par loy le menrres."
(ll. 6019-26)
. . . si l'a aresnié:
"Leres qui mon signour mourdristes
Et en traÿson le feristes, . . .
Vous seres demain traÿnés,
Comme mourdreres fel prouvés."
Dist Sones: "Vous aves menti,
Ains lui ne autrui ne traï.
Che sache Dieus, se je l'ocis,
Sour mon cors deffendant le fis.
Au roy de Noreweghe estoie
Et con saudoijers le siervoie.
Il vint et sour lui et sour mi,
A mon pooir nous deffendi.
Autrui vint grever pour conquerre,
Et si vint sour nous sa mort querre.
Et je l'ocis comme preudom,
Et si eut bonne raison.
Ne mais mourdreres chilz seroit
Qui pour ce fait mal me feroit.
Et sachies bien tout entresait,
Se vous nul mal m'en avies fait,
Que chialz qui sont enprisonné
Averies a leur mort mené."
Et dist li baillieus: "Fel boisiere,
Prouvé est que t'es mourdrissiere.
Bien sachies que vous en morres
Se vous par loy n'en escapes."
Li mestres templiers respondi:
"Pour loy prendre l'amenay chi.
Or en faites la loy jugier
Con de haut homme saudoijer."
Dist li baillieus: "Or le wardes,
Les pers dou castiel ay mandés.
Le matin par loy le menrrons,
Apriés si le traÿnerons."
(ll. 6048-84)
Li pers dou castiel sont venu
Et au temple sont descendu.
(ll. 6087-8)
Li haus baillieus mout haut parla,
Voyant tous Sone demanda:
"Mourdreres, en aves mourdri
Le bon roy cui tierre ch'est ci?"
Dist Sones: "Je n'en mourdri mie,
Con preudon li toli la vie
Pour mi et mon signour sauver,
Cui il venoit desireter;
Si l'ochis en son paveillon
A plain jour devant maint baron.
Et bien l'offre a moustrer du cors.
Mourdre et traÿson par est fors."
A tant va son gage baillier,
Selonc ce rouva il jugier.
Li uns pers l'autre a regardé,
Li baillieus lor a commandé
Que il le mourdrëur jugaissent,
Par jugement lui delivraissent.
Li per dïent qu'il jugeront
Selonc droit, ja tort n'i feront.
Dist li baillieus: "Vous jugeres,
S'escouterai que vous dires."
A tant en une cambre en vont
Chil ki de fief jugëour sont,
S'ont ensanle mout devisé
Et de maint jugement parlé.
Mais ains n'i ot .I. si felon
C'a Sone tournast traÿson.
Jugement ne pueent trouver,

Dont par droit le puissent grever.
En Noruëghe ont leur amis
Qu'en maint lieu an en prison
mis.
Se il faus jugement faisoient,
Tout lor ami pis aroient.
Et dist li uns: "Car en alons
Et sauf jugement li portons."
Li pers dïent: "Dont li portes
Mout volontiers, se vous voles."
Chieus dist qui pour yalz doit
parler:
"Sire, or nous faites escouter,
Nous avons ensanle parlé.
Chilz hons a no signour tué.
Si disommes no jugement.
S'il avoit tant de hardement
Qu'il se vosist a .II. combatre,
Se vaintre les puet et abatre,
Tous sains et saus il s'en ira
Et tout chil qu'il amené a.
Et conduis lui sera livrés,
Tant qu'a bon port soit arrivés.
Traÿnés seroit et pendus,
Se par ces .II. estoit vaincus. . ."
(ll. 6093-6144))

46. Although the episode in question takes place in Ireland, the legal background is probably not Irish but French, for, with the exception of what appears to be Norwegian non-legal custom in *Sone de Nansai,* Nyrop ("*Sone de Nansai* et la Norvege," *Romania,* XXXV, 555) says of French romances in general: "Les us et coutumes, les villes et leur population, les châteaux et les bourgs, la vie publique et familiale, la nature et les paysages tout est français. . . . " And in speaking of the *chansons de geste* Gautier ("L'Idée politique dans les chansons de geste," p. 100) criticizes the poets for making the Saracen institutions and customs too much like those of the French.

47. By way of contrast the *chanson de geste Floovant* presents a situation turning upon a law like that of Abbeville, for even the man who kills in self-defense admits his error.

The squire Richier, attacked by three brothers, kills the youngest. At night he stays at the home of Emelon, father of the three knights. When the host learns that the guest has killed his son, against all rules of hospitality he attacks Richier, who, reminding him of his indiscretion, admits the killing, asserting, however, that the son had struck the first blow, and suggesting in view of the unusual circumstances a combat with Emelon to decide the question at stake. In Richier's prayer before the combat, one utterance is significant. He says. "Bien sai que je ai tort, certes et il ai droit" (l. 1129). And even the poet in his solicitude wishes that "Dex aït Richier, car Emelons ai droit" (l. 1172).

48. Mar vëistes la mort mon frere,
Car vos li tolistes la vie
Al tournoi de Roche Florie.
Or vos ferai mout de mal traire,
A chevaus deronpre et detraire;
. . .
Longement girés en prison. . .
Et quant je vos arrai detrait,
Dont serés ars sans nul retrait,
Aprés ert ventee la polre; . . .
(ll. 7396-7419)

49. *Coutumes,* 1957: Aucune fois avient il que jeus est commenciés si comme pour behourder, ou pour çouler, ou pour jouer as barres, ou pour autres jeus, et avient qu'aucuns est tués ou afolés pour le jeu par ce qu'il

est encontrés contre le cuer, ou que la lance le tue, et en aucune autre maniere. Et quant tele chose avient, l'en n'en doit riens demander a celi qui le fist, car jeu qui est commenciés pour jouer sans malveillance et il mesavient du jeu par mescheance, nule justice n'en doit estre prise. Mes autrement iroit s'il se couroucoient en jouant, si que li fes fust fes par le courous, car en tel cas cil seroit justiciés qui le feroit, pour le mesfet; car si tost comme li courous vient, li jeus faut.

50. Lines 21797ff.

51. Lines 51-60.

52. Li cuers de joie li sautele,/C'or pense acomplir son desir/De son seignor qu'll veut murdrir (ll. 218-20).

53. Amors fet mainte chose fere/Qui torne à mal et contrere;/Nus ne puet vers li contrester; . . . (ll. 5687-89).

54. For example, Chrétien's *Charette* (ll. 2793-2953), in which a knight begs Lancelot for his life while a damsel demands his death. In order to satisfy both, Lancelot grants the vanquished his life, but makes him fight a second time. Lancelot easily conquers the man again, this time, however, beheading him to please the damsel.

Chapter V

1. Cf. M. Schlauch, *Chaucer's Constance and Accused Queens*, pp. 5, 6, 9, 11, 13, 20, 25, 26, 29, 30, 32, 33, 34, 46, 60, 61, 62, 63, 76ff., 86ff., 100, 103, 107 n. 113.

2. *Ibid.*, p. 98ff.

3. "L'Idée politique dans les chansons de geste," p. 100.

4. "The Character Types in the Old French Chansons de Geste," PMLA, XXI, 341, 345.

5. Comfort implies something of this idea when he says ("The Essential Difference between a *Chanson de Geste* and a *Roman d'Aventure*," PMLA, XIX, p. 70): "The traitor, as an active personage, is foreign to the romances and is a conventional and persistent type of an historical original, preserved only in the *chansons de geste*." Miss Barrow (*The Medieval Society Romances*, p. 85f.) although stressing conventionality of character in the romances, notes also that, on the whole, action in the romances is adequately motivated (p. 68).

6. Cf. G. Paris, "Le Roman du Comte de Toulouse," *Annales du Midi*, XII, 12, n. 1.

7. *Souniou Breiz-Izel*, II, 203ff.

8. Méon, *Nouveau recueil de fabliaux et contes*, I, 192ff.

9. *The Medieval Society Romances*, pp. 68-69.

10. Miss Barrow's note (*op. cit.*, p. 70, n. 1) is as follows: "The *Joufrois* and *Gawain and the Green Knight*, though society romances by virtue of their attention to social setting and their aristocratic appeal, are not sufficiently concerned with *fine amor* to show the common formula."

BIBLIOGRAPHY

BIBLIOGRAPHY

Abbreviations

APF Anciens poètes de France
BLVS Bibliothek des literarische Vereins Stuttgart
GRL Gesellschaft für romanische Literatur
PMLA Publication of the Modern Language Association
SATF Société des anciens textes français
SHF Société de l'histoire de France

Primary Sources

The name of the editor, translator, or compiler immediately follows the title.

Achery, Jean L. d', Spicilegium. 3 vols. Paris, 1723.

Adenet le Roi, Cléomadés. André van Hasselt: Li roumans de Cléomadés, par Adenés li Rois. 2 vols. Bruxelles, 1836-38.

Albertus Magnus, Liber de muliere forte, vol. 18, opera omnia. P. P. Quétif and Echard. Paris, 1890-99.

Amadas et Ydoine. Célestin Hippeau. Paris, 1863

Amis et Amilum. Eugen Kölbing. Heilbronn, 1884.

Aquinas, Thomas, Summa theologica. Translated by The Fathers of the Dominican Province. Three parts in 19 vols. London, 1911-25.

Assises de Jerusalem. Arthur A. Beugnot. 2 vols. Paris, 1841-43.

Athelston. Julius Zupitza. "Englische Studien," XIII, 1899.

Beaumanoir, Philippe de Remi, Sire de, Coutumes de Beauvaisis. Amedée Salmon. 2 vols. Paris, 1899-1900.

——— La Manekine. Hermann Suchier: Oeuvres poétiques de Beaumanoir. 2 vols. Paris, 1884-85. SATF.

Blancandin. Henri Michelant. Paris, 1867.

Bracton. De legibus et consuetudinibus Angliae. Text and translation, Travers Twiss. London, 1879.

Britton. Text and translation, Francis M. Nichols. 2 vols. Oxford, 1865.

Caesar, Julius, De bello Gallico. John H. Westcott: The Gallic War. New York, 1902. Translated by W. A. Macdevitt. "Everyman's Library," 1929.

Caesarius of Heisterbach, The Dialogue on Miracles. Translated by H. von E. Scott and C. C. Swinton Bland. London, 1929.

Chastelaine de Vergi. G. Raynaud. Paris, 1910.

Châtelain de Coucy. Georges A. Crapelet. Paris, 1829.

Chrétien de Troyes, Chevalier de la charette, Cligés, Erec, Yvain. Wendelin

Foerster: Christian von Troyes, sämtliche erhaltene Werke. Halle, 1884-99. Translated by William W. Comfort. "Everyman's Library," 1914.
Claris et Laris. Johann Alton: Claris und Laris. Tübingen, 1884. BLVS.
Comte de Poitiers. Francisque Michel. Paris, 1831.
Coutumes et institutions d'Anjou et du Maine. Charles J. Beautemps-Beaupré. 8 vols. Paris, 1877-97.
Durmart le galois. Edmund Stengel. Tübingen, 1873. BLVS.
Erle of Toulouse. Joseph Ritson: Ancient English Metrical Romances, III, 3d. ed. London, 1802.
Établissements de Saint Louis. Paul Viollet. 4 vols. Paris, 1881-86. SHF.
Eustace le moine. Wendelin Foerster and J. Trost. Halle, 1891.
Flamenca. Paul Meyer. Paris, 1865.
Floovant. François Guessard and H. Michelant. Paris, 1859. APF.
Florence de Rome. Axel Wallensköld. 2 vols. Paris, 1909. SATF.
Floriant et Florete. Francisque Michel. Roxburghe Club, Edinburgh, 1837.
Gautier d' Arras, Ille et Galeron. Wendelin Foerster: Walter von Arras, Ille et Galeron. Halle, 1891.
Gautier de Tournay, Gilles de Chin. Frédéric Reiffenberg. Bruxelles, 1847. Monuments pour servir à l'histoire des provinces de Namur, de Hainaut, et de Luxembourg.
Gerbert de Montreuil, Le Roman de la violette. Douglas L. Buffum. Paris, 1928. SATF.
Glanvill, De legibus et consuetudinibus regni Angliae. George E. Woodbine. New Haven, 1932. Translated by John Beames, Washington, D.C. 1900.
Godefroy de Paris. Chronique métrique. Jean A. Buchon. Paris. 1827.
Gregory of Tours, History of the Franks. Translated by Ormonde M. Dalton. 2 vols. Oxford, 1927.
Gui de Bourgogne. François Guessard and H. Michelant. Paris, 1858. APF.
Guillaume de Palerne. Henri Michelant. Paris, 1876. SATF.
Guillaume le clerc, Fergus. Ernst Martin. Halle, 1872.
Horne, Andrew, Mirroir de Justices. William J. Whittaker (translated by William Hughes). London, 1895. Selden Society.
Jehan Renart, Guillaume de Dole. Gustave Servois. Paris, 1893. SATF.
Joinville, Jean, Sire de, Histoire de Saint Louis. Joseph N. de Wailly. Paris, 1858. Translated as Chronicle of the Crusades by F. Marzials. "Everyman's Library," 1926.
Jostice et de plet. Luigi N. Rapetti. Paris, 1850.
Joufrois. Konrad Hofmann and F. Muncker. Halle, 1880.
Macaire. François Guessard. Paris, 1866. APF.
Maillart, Jehan, Le Roman du Comte d'Anjou. Mario Roques. Paris, 1931.
Méon, Dominique M., Nouveau recueil de fabliaux et contes. 2 vols. Paris, 1823.
Olim, Les. Arthur A. Beugnot. 3 vols. Paris, 1839-48.
Ordericus Vitalis. Historiae ecclesiasticae. Augustus le Prevost. 5 vols. Paris, 1838-55. SHF.

Parise la Duchesse. François Guessard and L. Larchy. Paris, 1860. APF.
Perlesvaus. William A. Nitze and T. A. Jenkins: Le haut livre du graal; Perlesvaus. 2 vols. Chicago, 1932-37. High History of the Holy Grail, Translated by Sebastian Evans. "Everyman's Library," 1929.
Philippe de Mousket, Chronique rimée. Frédéric Reiffenberg. 2 vols. Bruxelles, 1836-38.
Pierre de Fontaines, Conseil à un ami. Ange I. Marnier. Paris, 1846.
Poetic Edda. Translated by Henry A. Bellows. New York, 1926. American Scandinavian Foundation.
Raoul de Houdenc, Meraugis de Portlesguez. Mathias Friedwagner: Raoul de Houdenc, sämtliche Werke. Halle, 1897.
Richars li biaus. Wendelin Foerster. Vienna, 1874.
Rigomer. Wendelin Foerster and H. Breuer: Les Mervelles de Rigomer, von Jehan. 2 vols. Dresden, 1908-15. GRL, 19, 39.
Robert le Diable, Roman de. Eilert Löseth. Paris, 1903. SATF.
Sone de Nansai. Moritz Goldschmidt: Sone von Nausay. Tübingen, 1899. BLVS.
Soniou Breiz-Izel. François M. Luzel. Paris, Bouillon, 1890.
Summa de legibus. Ernest J. Tardif. Rouen and Paris, 1896.
Tacitus, Germania. Rodney P. Robinson. Middletown, Conn., 1935. American Philosophical Association Monograph No. 5.
Thomas, Tristan. Joseph Bédier: Le Roman de Tristan, par Thomas. 2 vols. Paris, 1902-5. SATF.
Très ancien coutumier de Normandie. Ernest J. Tardif. Latin, Rouen, 1881; French, Rouen, 1903.
Yder. Heinrich Gelzer. Dresden, 1915. GRL, 31.

Secondary Sources

Amira, Karl von, Die germanischen Todesstrafen. München, 1922.
Baist, G., "Der gerichtliche Zweikampf, nach seinem Ursprung und im Rolandslied," *Romanische Forschungen*, V.
Bar, Ludwig, History of Continental Criminal Law. Translated by T. S. Bell. Boston, 1916.
Barrow, Sarah F., The Medieval Society Romances. New York, 1924.
Bechis, Michael, Repertorium biblicum totius sacrae scripturae concordantiae. 1899
Bédier, Joseph, and P. Hazard, Histoire de la littérature française illustrée. 2 vols. Paris, 1923-24.
Boca, Jean, La Justice criminelle de l'echevinage d'Abbeville au moyen âge 1184-1516. Lille, 1930.
Bouvier, John, Law Dictionary. F. Rawle's 3d unabridged revision (8th ed.). Kansas City, 1914.
Briffault, Robert, The Mothers. 3 vols. New York, 1927.
Brissaud, Jean B., A History of French Public Law. Translated by J. W. Garner. Boston, 1915.

Brooke, Zachary N., The English Church and the Papacy. Cambridge, England, 1931.

Bruce, James D., The Evolution of Arthurian Romance from the Beginnings down to the Year 1300. 2 vols. Göttingen, 1923-28.

Brunner, Heinrich, Deutsche Rechtsgeschichte. 2 vols. Leipzig, 1892. 2d ed., 1906-28.

——— "Ueber absichtlose Missethat im altdeutshen Strafrechte," Forschungen zur Geschichte des deutschen und französischen Rechtes, X. Stuttgart, 1894.

——— Wort und Form im altfranzösischen Process, "Sitzungsberichte der philosophisch-historischen Classe der kaiserlichen Akademie der Wissenschaften," LVII. Wien, 1867.

Cauwenbergh, Étienne van, Les Pélèrinages expiatoires et judiciaires dans le droit communal de la Belgique au moyen âge. Louvain, 1927.

Chénon, Émile, Histoire générale du droit public et privé. 2 vols. Paris, 1926.

Comfort, William W., "The Character Types in the Old French *Chansons de Geste*," PMLA, XXI, 279ff.

——— "The Essential Difference between a *Chanson de Geste* and a *Roman d'Aventure*," PMLA, XIX, 70f.

Coulin, Alexander, Der gerichtliche Zweikampf im altfranzösischen Process. Berlin, 1906.

Delachenal, Roland, "De l'avocat dans la littárature du moyen âge." Histoire des avocats au parlement de Paris, chap. xvi, pp. 299ff. Paris, 1885.

Delattre, Edmond, Recherches sur le droit pénal à Cambrai et dans le Cambresis au moyen âge. Lille, 1929.

Delcourt, André, La Vengeance de la commune, l'arsin, et l'abattie de maison en Flandre et en Hainaut. Lille, 1930.

Dickson, Arthur, Valentine and Orson. New York, 1929.

DuCange, Glossarium mediae et infimae latinitatis. Paris, 1845.

Esmein, Adhémar, History of Continental Criminal Procedure. Translated by J. Simpson. Boston, 1913.

——— Cours élémentaire d'histoire du droit français. Paris, 1908.

Euler, Heinrich. Recht und Staat in den Romanen von Christian von Troyes. Marburg, 1906.

Foerster, Wendelin, "Der Feuertod als Strafe in der altfranzösischen erzählenden Dichtung," "Studien zur englischen Philologie." Halle, 1913.

Fournier, P., Les Officialités du moyen âge. Paris, 1880.

Fundenberg, George B., Feudal France in the French Epic. Princeton, 1918.

Gautier, Léon, Chivalry. Translated by H. Frith. London, 1891.

——— Les Epopées françaises. 5 vols. Paris, 1878-97.

——— "L'Idée politique dans les chansons de geste," *Revue des questions historiques*, VII.

Glasson, Ernest, Histoire du droit et des institutions . . . d'Angleterre. 6 vols. Paris, 1882-83.

——— Histoire du droit et des institutions de France. 8 vols. Paris, 1887-1903.

Goebel, Julius, Jr., Felony and Misdemeanor. New York, 1937.

Grelewski, S., La Réaction contre les ordalies en France depuis le IXe siècle jusqu'au décret de Gratien. Rennes, 1924.

Grimm, Jacob, Deutsche Rechtsalterthümer. 2 vols. Leipzig, 1899.

Guilhiermoz, Paul, Essai sur l'origine de la noblesse en France. Paris, 1902.

Gundolf, Friendrich, The Mantle of Caesar. Translated by J. W. Hartman. New York, 1928.

Hibbard, Laura A., Medieval Romance in England. New York, 1924.

His, Rudolf, Deutsches Strafrecht bis zur Karolina. München and Berlin, 1928.

——— Das Strafrecht des deutschen Mittelalters. 2 vols. Leipzig, 1920-35.

——— "Totschlagsühne und Mannschaft." Berlin, 1910. Festgabe für Dr. Karl Güterbock.

Holmes, Urban T., A History of Old French Literature from the Origins to 1300. New York, 1937.

Huganir, Kathryn, "Equine Quartering in *The Owl and the Nightingale*," PMLA, December, 1937.

Huizinga, Johan, The Waning of the Middle Ages. Translated by J. Hopman. London, 1924.

Junge, Adolf, Über Gerichtsbeamte und Gerichtsverhältnisse in der Litteratur des alten Frankreichs. Göttingen, 1906.

Kettner, Robert P., Der Ehrbegriff in den altfranzösischen Artusromanen. Leipzig, 1890.

Langlois, Charles V., La Vie en France au moyen âge. 2 vols. Paris, 1924.

——— Le Regne de Philippe III le Hardi. Paris, 1887.

Lawrence, William W., Shakespeare's Problem Comedies. New York, 1931.

Lea, Henry C., History of the Inquisition in the Middle Ages. 3 vols. New York, 1887-88.

——— Superstition and Force. Philadelphia, 1892.

Lear, Floyd S., "The Early History of Treason." Unpublished Harvard dissertation. 1925.

Le Foyer, Jean, Exposé du droit pénal normand au XIIIe siècle. Paris, 1931.

Leibecke, Otto, Der verabredete Zweikampf in der altfranzösischen Litteratur. Göttingen, 1905.

Lévitt, Albert, "Origin of the Doctrine of *Mens Rea*," *Illinois Law Review*, XVII, 1922.

Luchaire, Achille, Histoire des institutions monarchiques de la France sous les premiers Capétiens. Paris, 1891.

——— Social France at the Time of Philip Augustus. Translated by E. B. Krehbiel. New York, 1912.

Maitland, Frederic, Collected Papers. Edited by H. A. L. Fisher. 3 vols. Cambridge, 1911.

Matulka, Barbara, The Novels of Juan de Flores and Their European Diffusion. New York, 1931.

Mayer-Homberg, Edwin, Die frankischen Volksrechte im Mittelalter. 3 vols. Weimar, 1912.

Meynial, E., "Remarques sur la réaction populaire contre l'invasion du droit romain en France au XIIe at au XIIIe siècles," Mélanges Chabaneau. Erlangen, 1907.

Mitteis, Heinrich, Lehnrecht und Staatsgewalt. Weimar, 1933.

——— "Politische Prozesse des früheren Mittelalters in Deutschland und Frankreich," Sitzungsberichte der Akademie der Wissenschaften Heidelberg, philosoph-historische Klasse, XVI-XVII, 1927.

Norgate, Kate, England under the Angevin Kings. 2 vols. London and New York, 1887.

Nyrop, Kr., "Sone de Nansai et la Norvege," *Romania*, XXXV, pp. 555ff.

Paris, Gaston, "Le Roman du Comte de Toulouse," *Annales du Midi*, XII.

Perrot, Ernest, Les Cas royaux, origine et développement de la théorie au XIIIe et au XIVe siècles. Paris, 1910.

Pfeffer, M., "Die Formalitäten des gottesgerichtlichen Zweikampfs," *Zeitschrift für romanischen Philologie*, IX (1885).

Pollock, Frederick, and F. Maitland, History of English Law. 2 vols. Cambridge, 1899.

Powicke, Frederick M., The Loss of Normandy. Manchester, 1913.

Rezneck, Samuel, "Constructive Treason by Words in the Fifteenth Century," *American Historical Review*, April, 1928.

Schlauch, Margaret, Chaucer's Constance and Accused Queens. New York, 1927.

Schoepperle, Gertrude, Tristan and Isolt; A Study of the Sources of the Romance. 2 vols. Frankfurt am Main and London, 1913.

Schultz, Alwin, Das höfische Leben. 2 vols. Leipzig, 1889.

Seignobos, Charles, The Feudal Regime. Translated by E. W. Dow. New York, 1902.

Strayer, Joseph, The Administration of Normandy under Saint Louis. Cambridge, Mass., 1932. Medieval Academy of America.

Stubbs, William, Constitutional History of England. 3 vols. Oxford, 1891.

Tanon, Célestin, Histoire des justices des anciennes églises et communautés de Paris. Paris, 1883.

Tardif, Adolphe, Histoire des sources du droit français. Paris, 1890.

Vinogradoff, Paul, Roman Law in Medieval Europe. Oxford, 1929.

Voretzsch, Karl, Introduction to the Study of Old French Literature. Translated by F. du Mont. New York, 1931.

Waitz, Georg, Deutsche Verfassungsgeschichte. 8 vols. Kiel, 1874-80.

Wegele, Hermann, Zur geschichte der falschen Anschuldigung. Erlangen, 1892.

Wilda, Wilhelm E., Strafrecht der Germanen. Halle, 1842.

INDEX

INDEX

Bei Fragen zur Produktsicherheit wenden Sie sich bitte an:
If you have any questions regarding product safety,
please contact:

Walter de Gruyter GmbH
Genthiner Straße 13
10785 Berlin
productsafety@degruyterbrill.com